MCCULLOCH
v.
MARYLAND

Implied Powers

of the Federal Government

GREAT SUPREME COURT DECISIONS

Brown v. Board of Education
Dred Scott v. Sandford
Engel v. Vitale
Furman v. Georgia
Gideon v. Wainwright
McCulloch v. Maryland
Marbury v. Madison
Miranda v. Arizona
Plessy v. Ferguson
Regents of the University of California v. Bakke
Roe v. Wade
United States v. Nixon

Great Supreme Court Decisions

MCCULLOCH v. MARYLAND

Implied Powers
of the Federal Government

Samuel Willard Crompton

CHELSEA HOUSE
PUBLISHERS
An imprint of Infobase Publishing

McCulloch v. Maryland

Chelsea House
An imprint of Infobase Publishing
132 West 31st Street
New York, NY 10001

ISBN-10: 0-7910-9262-3
ISBN-13: 978-0-7910-9262-0

Library of Congress Cataloging-in-Publication Data
    Crompton, Samuel Willard.
    McCulloch v. Maryland : implied powers of the federal government / Samuel Willard Crompton.
       p. cm. — (Great Supreme Court decisions)
    Includes bibliographical references and index.
    ISBN 0-7910-9262-3 (hardcover)
    1. McCulloch, James W.—Trials, litigation, etc.—Juvenile literature. 2. Maryland—Trials, litigation, etc.—Juvenile literature. 3. Bank of the United States (Baltimore, Md.)—Trials, litigation, etc.—Juvenile literature. 4. Banks and banking, Central—Law and legislation—United States—History—19th century—Juvenile literature. 5. Exclusive and concurrent legislative powers—United States—History—19th century—Juvenile literature. 6. State rights—History—19th century—Juvenile literature. I. Title. II. Title: McCulloch versus Maryland. III. Series.
    KF228.M318C76 2007
    346.73'08211—dc22   2006023242

Chelsea House books are available at special discounts when purchased in bulk quantities for businesses, associations, institutions, or sales promotions. Please call our Special Sales Department in New York at (212) 967-8800 or (800) 322-8755.

You can find Chelsea House on the World Wide Web at http://www.chelseahouse.com

Text design by Erika K. Arroyo
Cover design by Takeshi Takahashi

Printed in the United States of America
Bang EJB 10 9 8 7 6 5 4 3 2 1

This book is printed on acid-free paper.

All links and Web addresses were checked and verified to be correct at the time of publication. Because of the dynamic nature of the Web, some addresses and links may have changed since publication and may no longer be valid.

· EQUAL · JUSTICE · UNDER · LAW ·

Contents

1

Black Dan

Daniel Webster stepped forward. It was March 1818 and he stood before the Supreme Court to argue the case of *Trustees of Dartmouth College versus William Woodward*, which everyone abbreviated to *Dartmouth v. Woodward*, or even more simply as the *Dartmouth* case.

Born in New Hampshire in 1782, Webster was 36 years old. He represented Massachusetts as a congressman, and he often pointed out that it was convenient for him that the Supreme Court met in the bowels (bottom floor) of the House of Representatives. Many a time Webster was able to hear or participate in a congressional debate, then hasten downstairs to appear before the Supreme Court.

Massachusetts congressman Daniel Webster, shown in this portrait circa 1851, argued more cases before the U.S. Supreme Court than anyone in history.

Though he was only 36, Webster was already on the way to becoming the most celebrated attorney in the history of the Supreme Court; during a long life, he would argue a total of 168 cases before it, more than anyone else, before or since. In 1818, he had already developed a handful of "trademarks," which let everyone know it was Daniel Webster speaking before the Court.

On that day in March, he wore a sparkling blue coat and high starched collar. The blue was offset by his black trousers, which he knew called attention to his handsome dark looks: not for nothing was he called "Black Dan." Webster had a distinctive way of speaking, starting slow and even soft, but building over the course of hours to a roll like thunder. He also stood distinctively, with one hand resting on a book or a sheaf of papers and the other hand held behind his back. As he warmed to his subject and his voice rose in power, Webster's hand would come from behind his back to make gesticulations to the Supreme Court judges (today we call them justices, but in the nineteenth century, they were "judges"). Webster used nearly every trick in the book; those who saw him in action thought him more brilliant than theatrical, more inspired than methodical. He was a model for most young lawyers of the time.

THE CASE

The facts of the *Dartmouth* case were as follows. In 1769, King George III had granted a royal charter to Dartmouth College, which was founded with an eye toward educating Native American boys. This original intent had not materialized and Dartmouth was attended largely by white Americans. The royal charter was out of date as soon as New Hampshire became one of the new United States, but the New Hampshire state government never took any action against the charter, or the college, until 1816. In that year, a new Republican governor and legislature tried to take over the college and rename it Dartmouth University. They argued that New Hampshire needed a public university and that the little college founded for Indian youths would fill a greater need by serving the people of the entire state.

It was difficult to argue with the premise that the people of New Hampshire needed more educational opportunities. As a son of the rocky soil of the Granite State, Daniel Webster knew very well how difficult it was for poor boys to get ahead (no one even thought about educating poor girls at the time). Webster had been lucky enough to attend Dartmouth himself; he was a graduate of the Class of 1801. Opposing feelings may well have tugged at Daniel Webster. He knew firsthand the lack of opportunities for education. Yet he was proud to be an alumnus of an exclusive academic institution. The $1,000 retainer he received from Dartmouth, together with the possibility of acquiring fame, also must have influenced Webster's thinking. By March 1818 he was ready to argue the case.

Chief Justice John Marshall and five other Supreme Court judges sat at the high bench. The Supreme Court was composed of a total of seven judges in those days, not the nine we know today, and one of the seven—Judge Todd of Kentucky—was absent on a regular basis.

Most people who knew John Marshall expected he would favor Daniel Webster and the Dartmouth College side of the case. Judge Marshall was famous for his belief in the sanctity of contracts, meaning that once an agreement was made in writing, it could not be revoked. Even so, Daniel Webster would have to put on a good show; there were five other judges to persuade.

Webster began slowly and calmly. He spoke of the importance of contracts in Anglo-Saxon law, referring to how England and its society had been governed by law ever since the time of the Magna Carta in 1215. Webster then spoke of the young United States. Born in 1782, he was just about the same age as the country that had taken form in the decade after it won independence from Great Britain. Webster cited plenty of case law, but he knew it would not be enough to win the case.

In 1818, Americans were divided between those who believed in states' rights and those who believed in the power of the national government. The former would naturally tend to agree with the State of New Hampshire, that the state government had the right to take over a college if need be. The latter would naturally side with Dartmouth College, saying that the sanctity of contracts was essential to keeping the nation probusiness. During his long career, Webster would sometimes argue one way and sometimes the other, but on this occasion he was 100 percent for Dartmouth College and the sanctity of contracts.

As he came to his conclusion, Webster's voice quaked a bit. Perhaps it was a lawyer's trick, perhaps he was caught by sincere emotion, but his voice almost broke as he came to the words that have remained famous ever since. Turning directly to look at Chief Justice John Marshall, Webster said, "Sir, you may destroy this little institution; it is weak, it is in your hands!"[1]

Webster went on to say that if the Court decided to let New Hampshire swallow up Dartmouth College, then it must be prepared to witness all colleges turn into political organizations. The pure pursuit of knowledge, he said, would be replaced by partisan bickering as the administration, faculty, and students of each college tried to curry political favor. He saved his best for last, saying, "It is, sir, as I have said, a small college. And yet *there are those who love it.*"[2] These 18 words form what is probably the most famous, and most often repeated part, of any argument before the Supreme Court. Webster had used logic well, and built to his logical conclusion, but he used emotion to sway the judges.

Shortly afterward, Webster wrote to a friend back home in New Hampshire. He was reasonably confident, he said, that the argument had won the day. Judge Marshall was clearly in favor, Judge Story seemed to be on their side, and one or two of the others would probably swing their way. No one ever knows the

Dartmouth College in Hanover, New Hampshire, was founded in 1769. Daniel Webster argued before the Supreme Court for the school to remain private.

result, however, until the Court makes it decision (many a TV courtroom drama builds its entire suspense up until the last few minutes, when the jury renders a verdict).

In this case, the result was an anticlimax. Judge John Marshall announced that the Court had heard several cases that judicial season, and that, given the importance of the Dartmouth case, it did not wish to render a hurried decision. Daniel Webster, Dartmouth College, and their opponents in the case would all have to wait until the opening of the 1819 judicial season to learn the results.

They would have to wait ten months. During that time period, though, another important case, that of *McCulloch v. Maryland*, would find its way to the Supreme Court.

EQUAL JUSTICE UNDER LAW

2

The Early Nation

The Supreme Court grew out of the competition between Federalists and Anti-Federalists. It rose from the troubled decade that launched the beginning of the American republic.

In May 1787, 55 men came to Philadelphia to design a new governing document for the land. The United States had won its political independence from Great Britain four years earlier, with the 1783 signing of the treaty of Paris, but the new nation had not consolidated or created a stable and lasting government.

There were many men and women who opposed the idea of a powerful central government. They remembered the tyrannies of King George III and believed Americans would do better with a system of state governments that would be sovereign

In the early days of the United States, Philadelphia was home to the nation's government. The Declaration of Independence and the U.S. Constitution were both created there. This print of the city was published in 1778.

unto themselves. This system had been in place since the Articles of Confederation were signed in 1781. Under the Articles, each state had the independent right to tax its citizens and make its laws. There was a weak federal government, located in Philadelphia, but it had neither the power to tax nor the power to compel. Thus began one of the great questions that would confound Americans until the end of the Civil War: Was the federal government sovereign, or were the individual states sovereign?

Sovereignty is defined as "supreme power, especially over a body politic."[3] This means that a sovereign power is the final power, the one that can override or overturn all others. The three branches of American government—legislative, executive, and judicial—are sovereign in all matters regarding the American people and the United States. To American minds in the twenty-first century, the Supreme Court is sovereign in regard to all judicial matters, but this was not always the case.

Fifty-five men came to Philadelphia, where they spoke, listened, and argued for the next four months. There were many brilliant men in that assembly, men like Alexander Hamilton, Gouverneur Morris, and Benjamin Franklin, but there were also some important men missing. At that time, John Adams was serving as the U.S. ambassador to Great Britain—the first American in that post—and Thomas Jefferson was the U.S. ambassador to France. Two of the best and the brightest men of their time did not get to participate in framing the Constitution.

THE FRAMING

It is well known that Alexander Hamilton, Gouverneur Morris, and a group of their followers wanted to create a strong federal government. Less is known about those in opposition; they believed that this new federal government would become a tyranny. It is hard to say what the common people of the time thought, for these 55 men alone had the power to draw up the new document. The people would have their turn a year later, when they could choose to accept or reject the new document outlining the powers of government.

By September, when their work was completed, the delegates had winnowed down to 38 men and their convention president, George Washington of Virginia. These 39 men signed the Constitution of the United States, which would not become the law of the land until it had been approved by three-fifths of the states. To put it briefly, the new document:

1. Separated the new government into three parts
2. Listed the legislative branch first, the executive branch second, and the judicial branch third
3. Delineated the powers and responsibilities of each branch

3. Created a set of checks and balances among the three branches

4. Left some confusion over which government was truly sovereign, the new federal one or those of the 13 individual states. (The word *sovereign* does not appear in the Constitution.)

 # THE BILL OF RIGHTS

Patrick Henry, James Madison, and other prominent Virginians did not stop championing state governments with the adoption of the Constitution of 1787. Believing in the rights of state governments, they worked to ensure that the people and the states had certain protections against the federal government.

The first 10 amendments to the Constitution were created together, passed by Congress and by two-thirds of the states, and signed into law in 1791. Together they are known as the Bill of Rights.

The Bill of Rights gives many specific protections to American citizens. The First Amendment protects freedom of speech, the second guards the right of the people to bear arms, and so forth. From a states' rights point of view, however, the most important section of the Bill of Rights is the Tenth Amendment, which reads, "The powers not delegated to the United States by the Constitution, nor prohibited by it to the States, are reserved to the States respectively, or to the people."*

This amendment did much of what Patrick Henry and others wanted, but it has never attained the status they hoped for. Even during the Civil War of 1861–1865, Southerners who fought for states' rights did not speak of the Tenth Amendment as much as they did of the original rights of states—the rights they had before the U.S. Constitution was even written.

---

* Shnayerson, Robert. *The Illustrated History of the Supreme Court of the United States.* New York: Abrams, 1986, p. 278.

The Constitution of the United States was drafted during secret sessions of the Constitutional Convention during the summer of 1787. The document famously begins, "We the People of the United States, in Order to form a more perfect Union, establish Justice, insure domestic Tranquility, provide for the common defense, promote the general Welfare, and secure the Blessings of Liberty to ourselves and our Posterity, do ordain and establish this Constitution for the United States of America."

This lack of certainty over sovereignty was not an oversight. Members of the Constitutional Convention were so divided over the issue that it made better sense to leave the issue undefined than to risk having the whole process come apart over it.

THE DEBATES

Soon after they left Philadelphia, the Framers had the document sent to each of the 13 states. Each state then appointed or elected delegates to a convention, which would either approve or reject the final document. No state had the power to alter or amend a single word, comma, or paragraph. The conventions could only give an up-or-down response.

Alexander Hamilton, John Jay, and James Madison worked hard to ensure New York would approve the document. They wrote anonymous articles in newspapers, which were later bundled together to form the *Federalist Papers*. Hamilton, Jay, and Madison argued that history showed that nothing less than a powerful central government could hold a nation together. If this was true of small countries like Spain or England, how much more true was it when 13 states, spread over the Atlantic seacoast, were concerned?

Their opponents put up counterarguments. The recent history of the Dutch Netherlands showed that seven independent provinces could join together and keep the nation going. The Dutch were fiercely protective of the independent liberties of their seven provinces, but they banded together when needed. There was also the successful example of Switzerland, which had been formed of separate cantons (local governments) for nearly five centuries.

The Federalists and Anti-Federalists made effective arguments. Generally speaking, it is safe to say that people involved with commerce (ships, banks, towns, and cities) were more in favor of a strong federal government, whereas those involved with agriculture (farms, land, animals, crops) tended to favor strong state governments and a weak federal one.

YOUNG MARSHALL

One could argue that John Marshall was never truly young, that he was too ambitious for that. Marshall also had a playful side, however, one that would emerge time and again over the years.

Born in 1755, he was the eldest of 15 children. His father was a successful "planter" in colonial Virginia, but the Marshalls definitely did not belong to what is called the "Tidewater aristocracy." In his short autobiographical sketch (which he wrote in about 1827), Marshall described his youth as greatly influenced by his father. They seem to have been the best of friends. Thomas Marshall was a self-made man, who imparted knowledge, wisdom, and ambition to his eldest son. John Marshall was translating from Latin by his teenage years; he also read widely in history and politics.

In 1775, the year the Revolution began, Marshall joined the Culpeper Minutemen. He took part in the first battle on Virginian soil, and later he switched units to join the Continental army. Continental army soldiers pledged to remain in the field until the war was won. He saw action at the battles of Brandywine Creek, Monmouth, and Stony Point. His presence contributed much to the cold winter at Valley Forge, where his good humor and athleticism (he was a champion runner) helped divert his fellow soldiers from their cold and hunger.

Marshall took time out in the spring and summer of 1780 to attend law lectures at the College of William and Mary: These few short months were all the advanced education he would ever have. He married Polly Ambler in 1783, and the couple settled in Richmond, Virginia, which would be Marshall's home base for the rest of his life.

By the time he went to the Virginia Convention of 1788, John Marshall had developed the reputation of a sharp-minded lawyer. He tended to favor men of property over others, and he was a firm believer in the sanctity of contracts.

The contest was heated in almost all the states, but Virginia proved a linchpin. Virginia was the most populous of the 13 states, and it also was home to many of the best public speakers of the time. There was Patrick Henry, who, in 1775, had shouted "Give me Liberty or give me Death!"; there was Edmund Randolph, who had played a big part in framing the Constitution; and there was George Wythe, properly considered the tutor of many brilliant men of the time. There was also young John Marshall, the sharp-minded lawyer who later became an important Supreme Court justice.

THE VIRGINIA CONVENTION

The Virginia Convention took place in Richmond, in the heat of early summer. Anyone from the North would have called for a quick adjournment, because of the intense heat, but these were Southern gentlemen, accustomed to their land and climate. Patrick Henry argued long and hard against the new Constitution, saying it smelled of monarchy. Under this system the states would be as much slaves to the federal government as they had been to King George III.

Many men spoke for the Consitution, and many men spoke against it, and the convention seemed undecided. No one expected John Marshall to play a leading role in defending the Constitution, but that is exactly what he did. Patrick Henry might easily have eclipsed Marshall in a legal arena. Henry was 20 years older and a far more practiced speaker. John Marshall had only practiced the law for the past five years, but he soon showed he had become a master:

> Mr. Chairman—I conceive that the object of the discussion now before us, is whether Democracy or Despotism, be most eligible. I am sure that those who framed the system submitted to our investigation, and those who now support it, intend the establishment and security of the former. The

John Marshall served as chief justice of the U.S. Supreme Court from 1801 to his death in 1835. Marshall shaped U.S. law and established the Supreme Court's right to judicial review in the landmark case *Marbury v. Madison*.

supporters of the Constitution claim the title of being firm friends of liberty, and the rights of mankind. They say, that they consider it as the best means of protecting liberty. We, Sir, idolize Democracy. Those who oppose it have bestowed eulogiums on Monarchy. We prefer this system to any Monarchy, because we are convinced that it has a *greater tendency* to secure our liberty and promote our happiness [italics added].[4]

A GREATER TENDENCY

Nothing was, or is, a sure thing. Any form of government can potentially lead the people to despotism. What the Founding Fathers had created in Philadelphia in 1787 was a system that would have a greater tendency to bring about the common good. John Marshall went on to explain why a strong federal government was needed:

We may derive from Holland lessons very beneficial to ourselves. Happy that country which can avail itself of the misfortunes of others—which can gain knowledge from that source without fatal experience! What has produced the late disturbances in that country? The want of a Government as is on your table, and having in some measure such a one as you are about to part with. The want of proper powers in the Government.[5]

John Marshall had become a Federalist. He and his fellows won the debate and the final vote. Virginia ratified the Constitution, which became the law of the land late in 1788.

EQUAL·JUSTICE·UNDER·LAW·

3

The Early Court

The Supreme Court is described in Article III of the Constitution:

> The judicial power of the United States, shall be vested in one supreme Court, and in such inferior Courts as the Congress may from time to time ordain and establish. The Judges, both of the supreme and inferior Courts, shall hold their offices during good behavior, and shall, at stated times, receive for their services, a compensation which shall not be diminished during their continuance in office.[6]

Nothing was said about the size of the Court or where it should hold session. These were matters that would be settled by congressional legislation. The Constitution was explicit about the powers of the new Supreme Court, however:

> The judicial power shall extend to all cases, in law and equity, arising under this constitution, the laws of the United States, and treaties made, or which shall be made, under their authority;—to all cases affecting ambassadors, other public ministers and consuls;—to all cases of admiralty and maritime jurisdiction;—to controversies to which the United States shall be a party;—to controversies between two or more states;—between a state and citizens of another state;—between citizens of different states;—between citizens of the same state claiming lands under grants of different states, and between a state, or the citizens thereof, and foreign states, citizens, and subjects.[7]

The wording is long, and, to our twenty-first-century ears, a little verbose, but the meaning is very clear: The Constitution gave sweeping powers to the Supreme Court. The Framers of the Constitution did not want a judiciary beholden to any other branch of government; they wanted one that would be sovereign unto itself. Many of the powers granted to the Supreme Court came from the minds and pens of men who believed in states' rights, for they believed a strong Supreme Court was one of the great defenders of states and their liberties. No one could predict exactly how the new Court would behave, though; in fact, it took some time before the Court even came together for its first session.

JUDICIARY ACT OF 1789

Congress moved to establish the federal judiciary in 1789. The Judiciary Act of that year divided the nation into three judicial districts, each of which would be tended to by two members of the Supreme Court (the Judiciary Act set the number of justices at six total, but this was changed to seven in the 1790s). The act also required the six judges to assemble in the nation's capital city (which then was New York) twice a year, at the beginning of February and the beginning of August.

 STATES' RIGHTS

The Eleventh Amendment reads, "The judicial power of the United States shall not be construed to extend to any suit in law or equity, commenced or prosecuted against one of the United States by citizens of another state, or by citizens or subjects of any foreign state."* From the moment the Constitution was created, there were those who argued it did not do enough to safeguard the rights of individual states.

Those who believed in states' rights—and there were many—thought that the new nation had been created by the people, but the people acting through the framework of their individual states. Those who believed in a strong federal government thought that the people had acted on their own, independent of what the states thought at the time. This great division of thought would last until the Civil War; indeed, it would be one of the major causes of the Civil War. Southern states, Virginia especially, argued for states' rights more than the Northern states did, but there were some exceptions. During the War of 1812, the five New England states (Maine was not yet separate from Massachusetts) considered some form of separation to prevent having to participate in a war they had opposed from the beginning. The New England delegates met at the Hartford Convention of 1814, prompting many other Americans to brand them as traitors.

People still care about states' rights today, but they do not speak with anywhere near the vehemence and certainty that they did in the first half of the nineteenth century.

---

* U.S. Constitution, reproduced in Peter Irons, *A People's History of the Supreme Court*. New York: Penguin Books, 1999, p. 495.

The Federal Judiciary Act of 1789 was one of the first acts of the new Congress, and it served to establish a federal court system.

THE FIRST JUDGES

Everyone knows that George Washington had a profound impact on the growth and development of the young republic. He was commander in chief during the Revolutionary War, leader of the convention that wrote the Constitution, and the first president of the United States. He also had the power—and this is much less recognized—to nominate a whole set of judges (or justices) who would set the tone for the early Supreme Court. The U.S. Constitution did not specify the number of judges for the Supreme Court, so the matter was decided by the Judiciary Act of 1789, which set the number at six.

Washington's first appointment went to John Jay of New York, whom he named chief justice. Born in 1745, Jay had been conservative as a young man. Practicing law from an early age, he was a Loyalist (or Tory) until about 1776, when he threw his lot in with the American revolutionaries. Afterward, he dedicated himself to serving the United States, whether as leader of the Second Continental Congress or as a diplomat to Spain. Because of his connections with finance and commerce, however, Jay remained a conservative (or a Federalist); as a Supreme Court judge, he was likely to defend the interests of property.

Washington also nominated John Rutledge of South Carolina, William Cushing of Massachusetts, James Wilson of Pennsylvania, John Blair of Virginia, and James Iredell of North Carolina. Washington started a practice of nominating men from different geographic parts of the nation, to lend a geographic balance to their proceedings. This precedent would be followed for many decades.

The Court met for the first time in the summer of 1790. The judges came together at the Royal Exchange Building in lower Manhattan, which served as the first headquarters for the nation's high Court. As there was no pressing business, it adjourned almost as soon as it came together.

This would seem like a ridiculously easy schedule were it not for the onerous burden of "circuit riding." Throughout the colonial period, judges had ridden horseback or taken carriages to remote rural areas, dispensing justice and acquainting common people with the workings of the law. This practice carried over to the new U.S. Supreme Court, whose members were obligated to go on what were sometimes six months of circuit rides. As early as 1792, the judges wrote to President

John Jay was the first chief justice of the United States. Jay was a member of the Continental Congress and later served as governor of New York.

Washington asking to be relieved of this duty: "We cannot reconcile ourselves to the idea of existing in exile from our families, and of being subjected to a kind of life, on which we cannot reflect, without experiencing sensations and emotions, more easy to conceive than proper for us to express."[8] In addition, the Judges also wrote to Congress:

> Some of the present Judges do not enjoy health and strength of body sufficient to enable them to undergo the toilsome journies through different climates and seasons, which they are called upon to undertake, nor is it probable that

SEAT OF GOVERNMENT

When the first president and the first Congress came together in 1789, New York City was the center of American government. George Washington took the oath of office there, Congress met there, and the first Supreme Court session, though brief, was held there.

In 1791, it was decided to move the seat of government to Philadelphia. Not only was that city more "moderate" in politics, but also it was closer to the geographical center of the country. The president, Congress, and Supreme Court all moved to Philadelphia that year, and it remained the center of American government until the spring of 1800.

Between 1791 and 1800, George Washington and others planned the new capital city to be built on the Potomac River between Virginia and Maryland. Washington played a large role in the planning, but agreements between Alexander Hamilton and Thomas Jefferson were essential in persuading other congressional leaders to make the move.

John and Abigail Adams were the first presidential couple to reside in the White House—they moved there in 1800, very late in his presidential term. Since then, Washington, D.C., has been the center of American political life.

any set of Judges however robust, would be able to support and punctually execute such severe duties for any length of time.[9]

Worst off by far was James Iredell of North Carolina. His Southern circuit rides took him through about 1,500 miles (2,414 kilometers) of travel each year, extending to the western side of the Appalachian Mountains, and all the way up and down the southern coast of the United States. Iredell looked hale and healthy when he was first chosen to serve on the Court, and he was one of the younger judges, but he was soon worn out from the burden of these long rides. Once he was mobbed, perhaps by people unhappy with a judicial decision, and once he was injured when his horses ran his carriage into a tree.

President Washington was sympathetic, but Congress was not. One leading congressman pointed out that if the judges remained in Philadelphia most of the time they would become vulnerable to the political vagaries that could cloud their judgment.

FIRST CASES

The Supreme Court heard far fewer cases in the 1790s than it does today. In the first year or two of its existence, the Court set about establishing procedures for the admittance of lawyers to the high Court. There were very few cases. The first truly big case the Court heard came in 1793.

During the Revolutionary War, the 13 different state governments had been at their wits' end to find money to participate in the war. They used many different strategies, including borrowing money from wealthy merchants. The case *Chisholm v. Georgia* involved one such merchant family. Chisholm was a stand-in for the heirs of a man who had given $70,000 (a great deal of money in those days) to the state of Georgia during the Revolutionary War. The heirs wanted the money back, and the state refused to pay.

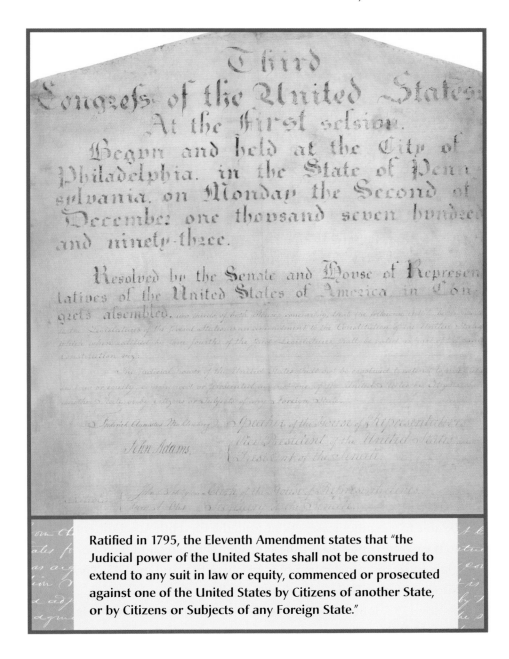

Ratified in 1795, the Eleventh Amendment states that "the Judicial power of the United States shall not be construed to extend to any suit in law or equity, commenced or prosecuted against one of the United States by Citizens of another State, or by Citizens or Subjects of any Foreign State."

The case found its way to the Supreme Court, where John Jay and three other justices ruled in favor of Chisholm. At that time in Supreme Court history, all the different justices issued their own written opinions. The custom of writing a unified Court opinion developed later, during the tenure of Chief Justice John Marshall.

As chief justice, John Jay took on a difficult question: Was a state suable? Many people believed that it was not. Americans were about equally divided between those who believed in the power of a strong federal government and those who argued for states' rights. Those of the latter persuasion found it easy to believe that an individual could not sue a state. Making matters worse, Chisholm was not a resident of the State of Georgia when he took his case to court.

Jay argued in the affirmative. Georgia, he said, was not sovereign in that it was dependent on and responsible to the federal government in Philadelphia (the government would not move to Washington, D.C., until 1800). Three other justices agreed with John Jay. They wrote long, extensive opinions in which they concurred that the heirs deserved some money, and Georgia would have to pay them. One justice, James Iredell of North Carolina, wrote a dissenting opinion.

Never since has a Supreme Court decision been so quickly overturned by the people. *Chisholm v. Georgia* raised a firestorm of opposition throughout the land. Georgia acted first, but the state was quickly joined by congressional leaders and most of the other states. No one wanted debts from the Revolutionary War to be collected. No one wanted individuals of one state to be able to sue other states. As a result, the Eleventh Amendment to the Constitution was rushed through the states and the Congress in record time; it became the law of the land in 1795. The Supreme Court had been severely rebuked.

By 1797, John Jay was no longer on the Supreme Court. He had always seen his post as temporary, and he resigned in 1795 to seek the governorship of New York (he won that race). After a short stint by South Carolina's John Rutledge, Oliver Ellsworth of Connecticut became the third chief justice of the Supreme Court. Nominated by President Washington and confirmed by the Senate, Ellsworth took his new place in 1796.

This 1887 portrait of Oliver Ellsworth was first published in *Century* magazine. Ellsworth is thought by some to have laid much of the groundwork of the accomplishments credited to John Marshall.

Today, it remains controversial as to whether Ellsworth was a good chief justice or a poor one. Some scholars maintain that many of the great changes wrought by John Marshall after 1801 were actually in the planning stage during Ellsworth's period as chief justice. The issue is difficult to resolve. Suffice to say that if Ellsworth was not particularly distinguished as chief justice, he certainly did not provoke any rebuke by the people, such as that created by John Jay with his decision in *Chisholm v. Georgia*. During Ellsworth's term the biggest complaint concerning the Supreme Court came from the justices themselves; they were weary from the many hours, days, and weeks of "circuit riding" through the American countryside.

As America entered a century, the 1800s, its people had good reason to be pleased with how the presidency and the legislature had performed. Few people had much to say about the Supreme Court, good or bad, though, because they knew so little about it. That would soon change. The Marshall era was about to commence.

4

The Court and Politics

When the new nation began in 1789, many people hoped that the Supreme Court would steer clear of political matters. President George Washington went further than this; he hoped that the president, Congress, and high Court would all steer clear of political partisanship. Of course, this was too much to ask for.

THE FIRST PARTIES

Political parties developed during the 1790s. Americans did not have a great deal of experience to draw on, so they looked to the British, who had long been divided between the Whigs and

Creator of the Federalist party, the first political party in the United States, Alexander Hamilton believed in a strong central government. Hamilton coauthored the *Federalist Papers*, which became a primary source for the interpretation of the U.S. Constitution.

Tories (the former tended to be from the middle- to upper-middle class and the latter tended to represent the interests of the titled aristocracy). Americans did not label themselves right away, but, through the leadership of Thomas Jefferson and Alexander Hamilton, they began to identify themselves as

Federalists or Anti-Federalists. (The Anti-Federalists renamed themselves the Democratic-Republicans, which was later shortened to simply Republicans.)

Born on the Caribbean island of Nevis, Alexander Hamilton came to New York City as a young man and made that place his lasting home. Brilliant with facts and figures, he rose in the Revolutionary Army and then as a Manhattan lawyer. By the time he participated in the framing of the Constitution, Hamilton was a confirmed Federalist, meaning that he believed in the necessity of a strong central government.

Hamilton believed that only a government with the authority to tax, and the power to collect those taxes, could really govern such a disparate group of people and places like the United States. Such a government had to have full sovereignty over the individual states. Implicit in Hamilton's argument was that mercantile cities like New York would provide the leaders and leadership for the new nation.

Thomas Jefferson believed just the opposite. Only 13 powerful state governments, each informed by the desires and needs of its citizens, could really govern such a large nation. Only state governments, with their ears to the ground, could really understand the needs of the people, and even state governments were not as truly sovereign as the people themselves. Implicit in Jefferson's argument was that the rural farmer was the backbone of the American republic.

President George Washington heard plenty from both men. Alexander Hamilton was secretary of the U.S. Treasury, and Thomas Jefferson was secretary of the U.S. Department of State. Washington was a bit in awe of both these men, who were better educated and were better speakers than himself, but he always reserved the final decision for himself. As a Virginian, we would expect him to side most often with Thomas Jefferson and the belief in the rural farmer, but over the years he tended to agree more with Hamilton and the cause of cities, industry, and finance.

THOMAS JEFFERSON,
Third President of the United States

Thomas Jefferson was an enemy and adversary of Alexander Hamilton. A believer in states' rights, Jefferson was against "big government."

By about 1793, the followers of Thomas Jefferson had become Republicans, and those of Alexander Hamilton had become Federalists. The two parties developed an intense dislike of each other, and the newspaper editorial pages were thick with anger and recrimination. Hamilton and Jefferson had started out as cautious friends, but by 1793 they had become bitter enemies. Then, making for even more dissension, came the events of the French Revolution.

Revolutionary France went to war with many of its European neighbors in 1793. Given that the French had helped the Americans win their revolution against Great Britain, the French Revolutionary government expected the United States to help it now. Thomas Jefferson argued in favor of the French cause, saying that the French were fighting for the rights and liberties of mankind. Alexander Hamilton argued that the French Revolutionaries had gone astray, and that it would be disastrous to help them. President Washington listened intently to both men, then made his own decision. America would remain neutral in the long Revolutionary and Napoleonic Wars.

 FROM MODERATE TO RADICAL

It is well known that King Louis XIV and Queen Marie Antoinette were both beheaded in 1793. Less known is that the French Revolution had started as a moderate movement.

In the summer of 1789, the long-suffering French people rose in revolt against their king and queen. The Bastille was stormed on July 14 (it has been the French national holiday ever since). The French Revolutionaries did not wish to topple the entire existing order, though; they wanted to work with the king and queen to establish a constitutional monarchy.

Louis XIV and Marie Antoinette were not bad people, but they were foolish. They conspired by letter with their relatives in Austria and planned to bring about an invasion of France to reestablish their absolute monarchy. In 1792, the king and queen tried to escape Paris and reach the Belgian border. They were recognized and caught just shy of their destination.

Brought back to Paris, Louis XIV and Marie Antoinette were put on trial. The king was found guilty by a majority, but, on the second vote, regarding whether he should be executed, the measure passed by exactly one vote. He went to the guillotine in January 1793, and Marie Antoinette followed later that year.

The executions of the king and queen transformed the French Revolution from a moderate movement into a radical one. Many Americans had hailed the beginning of the French Revolution, thinking it would model their own. The executions of 1793, though, and the continued use of the guillotine against high-placed French nobles, brought many Americans to loathe what was happening on the other side of the Atlantic.

American politics became even more divisive as Americans lined up on different sides concerning the French Revolution. By the time George Washington retired from public life in 1797, Americans had become deeply divided. There were Federalists, Republicans, and plenty of people who detested both political parties. In his farewell address, published in 1796, Washington warned the American people of the bitterness of party spirit; he hoped that parties would disappear in the future. That was a forlorn hope.

THE UNDECLARED WAR WITH FRANCE

John Adams became the second president of the United States in 1797. A leader of the Federalist Party, he attempted to follow what he believed had been George Washington's excellent example. Adams was bedeviled, though, by relations with Revolutionary France. In 1798, he sent three diplomats to Paris to try to work out a commercial treaty with the French government: Charles Cotesworth Pinckney, Elbridge Gerry, and John Marshall.

The three American diplomats were kept waiting a long time. The French Revolutionary government refused to receive them in public, but under the cover of night, three Frenchmen (named only as Misters X, Y, and Z) visited them at their hotel. No negotiations could be expected, they said, until the Americans paid a bribe of $250,000. This money must be paid to them before Foreign Minister Talleyrand would agree to see them. The American diplomats were outraged. Charles Pinckney is generally credited with having come up with the resounding answer: "No, we will not give you a six pence." This was later changed, by the American public, to "Millions for defense, but not a penny for tribute!"[10]

The three Americans went home, where they were received by rapturous crowds. John Marshall, who was then 43, had his first taste of national attention, and he enjoyed it. President Adams was reluctant to ask Congress for a declaration of war, so he authorized a limited naval war with France, which lasted for two years. The newly built USS *Constitution* and USS *Constellation* performed remarkably well in this conflict. The most lasting, and most bitter, effect of the undeclared naval war, however, was the creation of the Alien and Sedition Acts.

In 1798, Congress passed and President Adams signed these two acts. They made it more difficult for aliens (non-U.S. citizens) to remain in the country and also made it a crime for newspapers to criticize the government in this time of war. The second, the Sedition Act, created animosities that lasted for years.

THE COURT IN 1800

By 1800, the Supreme Court had emerged as a bastion for the Federalist Party. The first 11 nominations had been made by Federalist-leaning George Washington, and three more had been made by Federalist John Adams. Even today, George Washington holds the all-time presidential record, with 11 nominations. (President Franklin D. Roosevelt comes in second, with a total of 9.) By 1800, there were only Federalists on the Court, and they were determined to leave their mark.

Judge Samuel Chase of Maryland was the most outspoken member of the Court. While riding circuit in 1798, he officiated at the trial of John Fries, who had led a rebellion in Pennsylvania. Chase made it plain he detested Fries and expected the jury to find him guilty. Fries's lawyers gave up the effort, and he was found guilty and sentenced to death. President John Adams pardoned him, however, thereby preventing what might have been a national uproar. People remembered Judge Chase's stance at the trial, and he became the most unpopular member of the high Court.

At this time, too, the Court needed a new leader. Oliver Ellsworth stepped down as chief justice in 1800, leaving the most important spot open. President John Adams naturally wanted to appoint a Federalist to replace him, but this nomination proved much trickier than ones in the past.

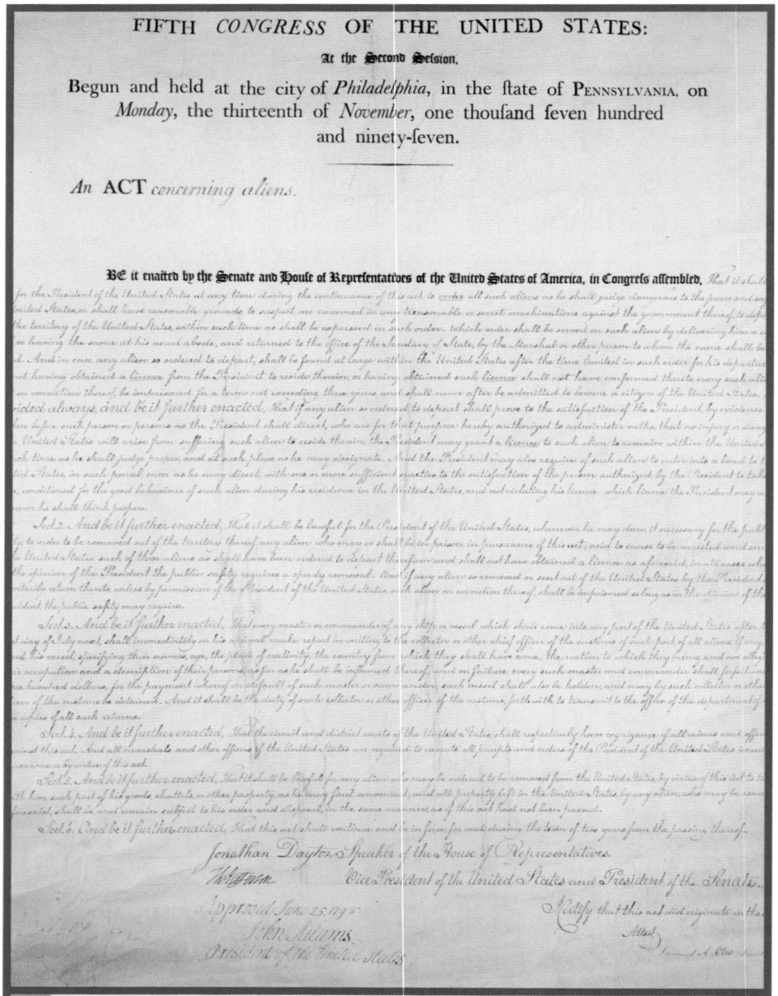
FIFTH *CONGRESS* OF THE UNITED STATES:

At the Second Session,

Begun and held at the city of *Philadelphia*, in the state of Pennsylvania, on *Monday*, the thirteenth of *November*, one thousand seven hundred and ninety-seven.

An ACT *concerning aliens.*

BE it enacted by the Senate and House of Representatives of the United States of America, in Congress assembled,

Jonathan Dayton Speaker of the House of Representatives.

Vice President of the United States and President of the Senate.

Approved June 25, 1798

John Adams

President of the United States

One of the earliest pieces of immigration legislation in the United States, the Alien and Sedition Acts were passed to reign in the liberties of foreign-born Americans and to limit free speech with regard to the government.

THE ELECTION OF 1800

John Adams ran for reelection in 1800. He had two major opponents, Thomas Jefferson and Aaron Burr. No one won enough states to win an outright majority in the Electoral

College, so the election was "thrown," per the U.S. Constitution, to the U.S. House of Representatives. The electoral ballots were cast in January, but the House took until the end of February to make its decision. Thomas Jefferson won the contested election of 1800.

Then as now, the U.S. government experienced a period called the "lame-duck" session, between the election of a new president and the date he actually takes office. Today, U.S. presidents are inaugurated on January 20, creating a lame-duck period of only two months. In 1800, however, the lame duck session extended from November until March 4, which was Inauguration Day. In those four months, President John Adams tried to stem the tide of Republican ascendancy.

Not only had Thomas Jefferson won the presidency, but his Republican Party had also won control of the Senate and House of Representatives. At that time, people did not have the type of confidence in the transition that we enjoy today—believing that one political party will replace another in an orderly and systematic fashion. Instead, there was a general fear, a panic even, that the incoming Republicans would wreck everything that George Washington, John Adams, and the Federalist Party had achieved over the past decade.

Given the anxiety that prevailed in his own party, John Adams decided to take strong action. In January 1801, he signed a brand-new Judiciary Act, which added to the one of 1789. Many new judgeships were created by this act, and President Adams took it upon himself to fill them.

Even more important, President Adams tried to leave the Supreme Court with a strong Federalist leader. At first he nominated John Jay, who had left the Supreme Court back in 1795, but when it became clear that Jay would refuse to serve, Adams turned to his secretary of state, John Marshall. In his autobiography, Marshall remembered it like this:

> When I waited on the President with Mr. Jay's letter declining the appointment he said thoughtfully "Who[m] shall I

This Currier and Ives portrait of John Adams shows the second president of the United States circa 1800. The Federalist Adams lost his bid for reelection in 1800, ushering in the Republican Party candidate Thomas Jefferson. Before Jefferson could take office, Adams left his mark on the government by enacting Federalist legislation and appointing representatives who would carry on his work.

nominate now?" I replied that I could not tell, as I supposed that his objection to Judge Patterson remained. He said in a decided tone, "I shall not nominate him." After a moment's hesitation he said "I believe I must nominate you."[11]

Remember that 26 years passed between the event and John Marshall's recollection. He continued:

> I had never before heard myself named for the office and had not even thought of it. I was pleased as well as surprised, and bowed in silence. Next day I was nominated, and although the nomination was suspended by the friends of Judge Patterson it was I believe when taken up unanimously approved.[12]

President Adams was acting from political motivations. So was John Marshall. Bringing John Marshall to the high court would change the nature of the Supreme Court and its place in American society. Marshall would remake the Court, and, in some ways, he would remake the nation.

5

The Marshall Court

When John Marshall became chief justice in 1801, the Court was 11 years old. During that time, it had decided a number of cases, including some important ones like *Chisholm v. Georgia*, but the Court had not fully entered into the hearts and minds of the American people.

This made sense. Americans, who were just starting to adjust to their political independence, were naturally more interested in the votes of Congress and the proclamations of the president than in the quiet deliberations of seven men. The newspapers reported the results of Supreme Court cases and sometimes even provided the contextual aspects of those decisions, but people were not greatly interested in the

46

Court, which seemed distant and removed from their ordinary lives. John Marshall and the Court he created would change this situation.

John Marshall was a very proud, determined man, one whom we could call "self-made." He had served with distinction in the Revolutionary War, and he rose in the legal profession in Virginia through his own efforts. By 1801, the year he became chief justice, Marshall had also become wealthy, due in part to having bought up large sections of land in Virginia that he knew from his boyhood. At the age of 46, he was determined, self-made, and an excellent example of American ingenuity. Though he was a native Virginian, and a distant relative of Thomas Jefferson, John Marshall was a committed Federalist. Unlike many of his Virginian neighbors, he believed, at least from 1788 on, that a strong central government was essential to the well-being of the republic. This belief put him in opposition to and conflict with many of his neighbors, who were Republicans and followers of Thomas Jefferson.

THE INAUGURATION OF 1801

On March 4, 1801, John Marshall rose early. As chief justice of the United States, it was his task to administer the oath of office to the incoming president, Thomas Jefferson. Though they were distantly related, the two men already disliked each other, a feeling that would only increase over the years.

Marshall administered the oath to Jefferson, who thereby became the third president of the United States. Jefferson began a lengthy and eloquent inaugural address, in which he asked his fellow citizens to remember that they were "all Federalists" and "all Republicans," that party animosities should not block their common status as Americans. While Jefferson gave the speech, however, Marshall and virtually every other Federalist in the crowd turned their backs on him. This was a bad start to what Jefferson hoped would be better, less antagonistic, times.

MARBURY V. MADISON

Soon after he came into office, President Jefferson learned that a number of commissions for judges had gone undelivered. As secretary of state (Marshall held that position as well as chief justice in February and March of 1801), it had been John Marshall's job to sign and deliver commissions to new federal judges and justices of the peace. Marshall had still been at his desk as late as 10:00 P.M. on March 3, but he had never completed the task, and a number of commissions remained unsigned and undelivered.

This was a boon for Jefferson, who deeply resented that outgoing President Adams had created these new judgeships in the first place. Jefferson ordered his new secretary of state, Virginian James Madison, not to deliver the remaining commissions, and there the matter sat for a while.

A handful of men who had expected to receive their commissions, however, sued in federal court. The most prominent of the group was William Marbury, of the District of Columbia, and the case that emerged became known as *Marbury v. Madison.*

In the winter of 1803, Chief Justice John Marshall found himself in the uncomfortable position of having to judge a case in which he had been a participant, for it was his failure to deliver the commissions that had brought about the case. Rather than recuse (disqualify) himself, John Marshall chose to be part of *Marbury v. Madison.*

Hundreds, if not thousands, of legal scholars have examined the decision in this case, and most have emerged with the conclusion that Marshall pulled off a judicial masterstroke. When it came time to write the decision, Marshall was under pressure from nearly all sides. He knew that if he ruled in favor of Marbury and ordered that the commission be delivered, President Jefferson would still refuse. That would make the Supreme Court look weak. On the other hand, if he ruled in favor of the federal government, the Court would look practically irrelevant.

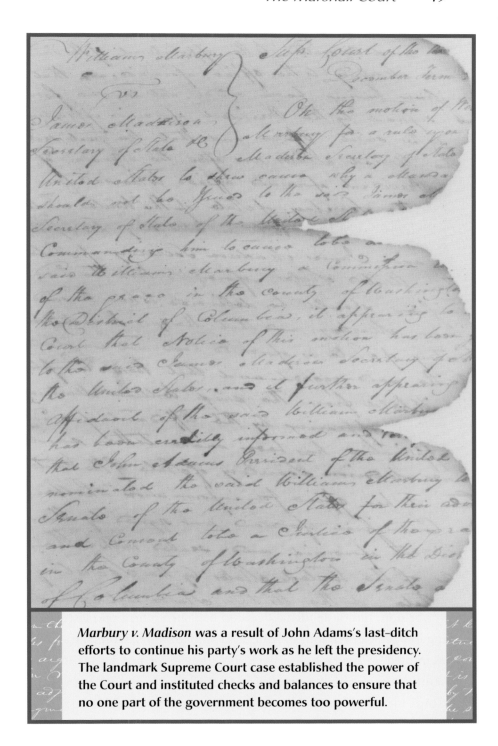

Marbury v. Madison was a result of John Adams's last-ditch efforts to continue his party's work as he left the presidency. The landmark Supreme Court case established the power of the Court and instituted checks and balances to ensure that no one part of the government becomes too powerful.

Marshall pulled off a magician's trick. He delivered the Court's decision in *Marbury v. Madison* in February 1803. The decision declared that: (1) William Marbury deserved his commission. (2) The Jefferson administration had done wrong in not delivering the commission. (3) The Supreme Court could not command the Jefferson administration to do so, because the high Court had only an appellate jurisdiction in this matter.

That should have been it. Marshall had decided that he and the Court lacked original jurisdiction, and they should have limited themselves to what has already been said. Here, however, John Marshall showed himself to be the supremely political judge that he truly was. Rather than leaving the matter as it was, John Marshall went one step further and announced that a section of the U.S. law code was unconstitutional.

In this early stage of national development, personal attributes, especially those of self-confidence, were sometimes more important than precedent or custom. Had a more timid man been chief justice in 1803, the Supreme Court might not have made its landmark decision in *Marbury v. Madison.*

Marshall ruled that Section 13 of the Federal Judiciary Act of 1789 was unconstitutional. That section appeared to give the Supreme Court power to do things like command the president to deliver a commission. Therefore, Marshall seemed to be acting in a humble manner, when in fact he was asserting the power of the Supreme Court to strike down a section of federal law.

Seldom has one judicial decision had such a firm and lasting impact. Generations of American scholars and lawyers have examined *Marbury v. Madison,* and they have not found it wanting. In one bold move, John Marshall moved the Supreme Court to a level at which it was roughly equal to Congress and the presidency. The battle was not over, however.

JEFFERSON STRIKES BACK

As mentioned earlier, Thomas Jefferson and John Marshall were distant cousins and fierce political enemies. President Jefferson was furious at Marshall for asserting the Supreme Court's power to strike down a section of federal law, and it was not long before Jefferson went on the offensive.

Early in 1805, Associate Justice Samuel Chase was impeached by Congress. Thomas Jefferson's Republican majority in Congress seemed ready to convict Chase of bad behavior as an associate justice, but they were thwarted by the poor performance of one of their congressional leaders. John Randolph of Roanoke (as he was called throughout his life) was a fierce Jeffersonian Republican, and a fine speaker, but he seems to have had an emotional meltdown during the impeachment proceedings. Randolph made a muddle of his prosecutorial arguments, and even the Republican majority in the Senate ruled in favor of Justice Chase. He was acquitted, and returned to the high Court.

Jefferson was an acute politician. He read the way the winds were blowing and decided that impeachment of a Supreme Court justice would not happen again during his administration. Privately, Jefferson lamented that his presidency was being limited, even crippled, by the will of the judges, whom no one had elected. In public, however, Jefferson and John Marshall were able to keep their tempers in check and remain civil to one another.

A LOOK AT THE HIGH COURT

One of the best descriptions of the Marshall Court appears in a letter written by a Massachusetts congressman. Joseph Story was in Washington, D.C., during the winter of 1808, and he wrote numerous letters home to one of his best friends, Samuel Faye of Massachusetts: "My dear friend, I have told you that I am frequently with the judges, and you will expect from me some touches at character painting. . . . The bench consists of Marshall, Chase, Cushing, Washington, Livingston, Johnson, and Todd."[13]

Story went on to describe all but Judge Cushing. "Marshall is of a tall, slender figure, not graceful nor imposing, but erect and steady. His hair is black, his eyes small and twinkling, his forehead rather low, but its features are in general harmonious. His manners are plain, yet dignified, and unaffected modesty diffuses itself through all his actions."[14] Many other observers attested to this description. Though he was a highly intelligent and highly ambitious man, John Marshall was personally of a modest disposition. This helps explain how he won over his fellow justices to his point of view on so many occasions. Story's letter continues:

> In conversation he is quite familiar, but is occasionally embarrassed by a hesitancy and drawling. His thoughts are always clear and ingenious, sometimes striking, and not often inconclusive; he possesses great subtlety of mind, but it is only occasionally exhibited. I love his laugh—it is too hearty for an intriguer—and his good temper and unwearied patience are equally agreeable on the bench and in the study. His genius is, in my opinion, vigorous and powerful, less rapid than discriminating, and less vivid than uniform in its light. He examines the intricacies of a subject with calm and persevering circumspection, and unravels the mysteries with irresistible acuteness.[15]

Joseph Story then turned his attention to Bushrod Washington, one of the associate justices of the Court. Bushrod was a nephew of George Washington. He lived at Mount Vernon, having inherited the late president's estate. Bushrod Washington and John Marshall thought alike to such an extent that some observers called them, simply, one judge. Story described Washington thus:

Washington is of a very short stature, and quite boyish in his appearance. Nothing about him indicates greatness; he converses with simplicity and frankness. But he is highly esteemed as a profound lawyer, and I believe not without reason. His written opinions are composed with ability, and on the bench he exhibits great promptitude and decision. It requires intimacy to value him as he deserves.[16]

Joseph Story then turned to Henry Brockholst Livingston:

Livingston has a fine Roman face; an aquiline nose, high forehead, bald head, and projecting chin indicate deep

George Washington's nephew Bushrod Washington was a Federalist and a Supreme Court justice, nominated by John Adams.

Henry Brockholst Livingston was appointed to the Supreme Court by Thomas Jefferson. Throughout his career, he consistently voted on the side of Chief Justice John Marshall.

research, strength, and quickness of mind. I have no hesitation in pronouncing him a very able and independent judge. He evidently thinks with great solidity, and seizes on the strong points of argument. He is luminous, decisive, earnest and impressive on the bench. In private society he is accessible and easy, and enjoys with great good humor the vivacities, if I may coin a word, of the wit and the moralist.[17]

No one can capture everything about another person on his or her first meeting. This is quite evident from Joseph Story's written assessment of Livingston. He may well have been charming in society, as well as witty, but Livingston also had a fierce temper. He fought three duels in his life and had killed a man in 1798.

Joseph Story then turned to the most truly controversial member of the high Court: Samuel Chase. Of him, Story said:

Of [Samuel] Chase I have formerly written. On a nearer view, I am satisfied that the elements of his mind are of the very first excellence; age and infirmity have in some degree impaired them. His manners are coarse, and in appearance harsh; but in reality he abounds with good humor. He loves to croak and grumble, and in the very same breath he amuses you extremely by his anecdotes and pleasantry. His first approach is formidable, but all difficulty vanishes when you once understand him. In person, in manners, in unwieldy strength, in severity of reproof, in real tenderness of heart; and above all in intellect, he is the living, I almost said the exact, image of Samuel Johnson. To use a provincial expression, I like him hugely.[18]

There could be no higher praise. The famous British lexicographer Samuel Johnson was legendary among Massachusetts intellectuals like Joseph Story. Once again, though, Story did not create his character portrait in its fullness. Samuel Chase was a high tempered and irascible man, whose judicial decisions had brought down upon him the anger of the Republican Party. In 1805, Samuel Chase had been impeached by Congress; he was acquitted after a lengthy trial.

South Carolina legislator William Johnson became the first Republican member of the Supreme Court.

Story continues with his description of William Johnson: "I ought not to pass by Judge [William] Johnson, though I scarcely know how to exhibit him individually. He has a strong mathematical head, and considerable soundness of erudition."[19] William Johnson was the first member of the Republican Party nominated and confirmed to the Supreme Court. He had been on the high Court for only two years at this point and had not yet been able to do what President Thomas Jefferson wanted: to inject a new Republican style of thinking into the Supreme Court.

Justice Thomas Todd was Story's next subject: "This is the first of Judge Todd's appearance on the bench, as he is a modest, retired man, I cannot delineate him. He does not appear to want talents."[20] Thomas Todd of Kentucky was the first man from west of the Appalachian Mountains to serve on the Supreme Court. Like William Johnson, he was from the Republican Party, and it was expected that he would try to swing his fellow judges in a new direction.

Although these descriptions are merely one man's opinion, Story's character sketches lend great insight into the Marshall Court.

6

The Country and the Bank

Thomas Jefferson left office on March 3, 1809, and was re-placed by his good friend James Madison, who became the fourth president of the United States. Seldom if ever has one president been able to leave the office to another and been so confident that his successor would follow his policies in the future. James Madison did not disappoint in this regard; but he, too, had to confront many of the things that had bedeviled Jefferson. One of these was the relationship between the presidency and the judiciary. Another, equally important one concerned the relationship between the United States and Great Britain. Yet another important question revolved around the Bank of the United States (BUS), which had been created in

James Madison was the fourth president of the United States. Madison continued Thomas Jefferson's work and ideologies, although unlike his predecessor he accepted the necessity of a national bank.

1791 and was about to come up for its recharter period. The government needed to decide whether to grant the bank a new 20-year charter.

James Madison took the problems one at a time. Regarding the Supreme Court, Madison was more conciliatory than

Jefferson had been. Madison thought the Supreme Court had overreached in the *Marbury v. Madison* decision, but he was willing to wait for an apt moment to try to reverse that situation. For the first years of Madison's administration, the president and the Supreme Court had relatively good relations.

Concerning the Bank of the United States, Madison was more pragmatic than Jefferson had been. Madison might not like the idea of a national bank, but he saw that that the BUS had been managed well during its first 18 or 19 years. Therefore,

BANK OF THE UNITED STATES

It had been controversial from the very beginning. In 1790, Secretary of the Treasury Alexander Hamilton had proposed a series of financial measures intended to improve the financial health of the young nation. One such measure was the creation of a national bank.

Opponents like Thomas Jefferson pointed out that the word "bank" does not appear in Article I of the U.S. Constitution, which delineates the powers and responsibilities of Congress. Many other Americans felt this way too; they felt that the federal government would acquire too much power by creating a national bank.

As was customary, President Washington listened to his two main policy advisors, Alexander Hamilton and Thomas Jefferson. The former was strongly in favor of a bank; the latter was strongly against one. President Washington came down on the side of Alexander Hamilton, who convinced Washington that the U.S. Constitution had "elastic" powers, meaning that Congress was not limited to the exact wording of Article I. The Bank of the United States (BUS) was formed in 1791, with a charter to run for the next 20 years.

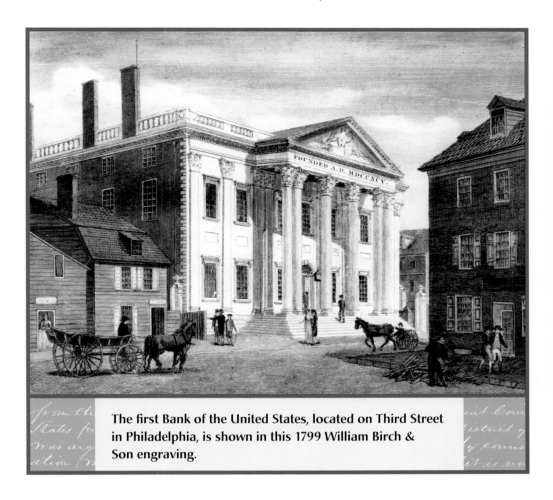

The first Bank of the United States, located on Third Street in Philadelphia, is shown in this 1799 William Birch & Son engraving.

President Madison did not voice any objection to a new charter for the BUS. Plenty of other people did, however.

THE RECHARTER ISSUE

As 1810 became 1811, Congress devoted a lot of time to the matter of the BUS. Even the fiercest critics of the BUS had to admit it had been well managed and that it had done some good for the country over the previous 20 years. Criticism, therefore, centered around the question of whether there was too much foreign influence.

Americans in the first decade of the century did not have much "ready cash," whereas many British merchants did. Therefore, much of the original stock of the BUS was in British hands. Many congressmen, especially the younger ones from the southern and western states, felt this was too great a foreign influence over American finances.

The older congressmen pointed out in vain that British investment in America was a good thing. If British merchants had thousands, indeed millions, of pounds sterling invested in America, they would pressure their government to stay at peace with the United States. Historian Henry Adams put it this way in his monumental history of the Jefferson and Madison administrations:

> Fully two thirds of the Bank stock, amounting to ten millions, were owned in England; all the five thousand shares originally subscribed by the United States government had been sold to England; and as the Bank was a mere creature of the United States government; these seven millions of British capital were equivalent to a score of British frigates or regiments lent to the United States *to use against England in war* [italics added].[21]

It did not matter. Southern and western congressmen led the charge against the Bank. This brought the matter to a tie vote in the U.S. Senate. Seventeen senators voted in favor of renewal and 17 voted against, thereby passing the matter to the hands of Vice President George Clinton.

Clinton had been an excellent governor of New York and had a keen financial mind, but he was embittered against his own administration. He and President James Madison did not see eye to eye. It was with some pleasure, therefore, that Vice President Clinton cast his vote in the negative and "killed" the Bank of the United States in February 1811. The bank was dead, but it would rise again.

The debates over the recharter of the Bank of the United States were, in many ways, the last hurrah for a number of older

A senator, congressman, and leader of the Whig Party, Henry Clay saw the importance of modernizing and building the U.S. economy. Clay's economic plan (called the American System) was designed to compete with British manufacturing and trade.

congressmen. Many went into voluntary retirement that year, whereas some others were swept out in favor of new, younger men. *Young* was the key word.

Henry Clay became Speaker of the House of Representatives when he was just over 30 years old. John C. Calhoun of South Carolina became a leading member of the "War Hawks," those who desired war with Great Britain, around the same time. Daniel Webster had not yet become a congressman, but his time was near. All these men would later play a role in the re-creation of the Bank of the United States.

VACANCIES ON THE COURT

Today a vacancy on the high Court almost means a political crisis. Republicans and Democrats alike strategize over how to confirm a nominee or defeat her or him. Examples of this type of political partisanship can be found in the stories of Judge Robert Bork in the 1980s, Justice Clarence Thomas in the 1990s, and others. In 1811, there were suddenly two vacancies on the high Court.

Justices Samuel Chase of Maryland and William Cushing of Massachusetts died in the same year. The two men had both been aged at the time of their deaths, and many people thought that the addition of younger men would enhance the high Court. Perhaps it is to this that Joseph Story owed his good fortune.

In January 1811, at about the same time Congress considered the BUS matter, President Madison put forward his nominee for the first Supreme Court vacancy. Judge Levi Lincoln of Massachusetts had been attorney general of the United States during the Jefferson administration, and he was well liked by men on both sides of the aisle. Lincoln turned the president and Congress down, however. He was old, and his eyesight was beginning to fail. It was time for him to retire to private life.

Madison was in a quandary. He wanted to replace the deceased Justice Cushing with a Republican, but there were few notable Republicans in New England (custom at the time demanded that a replacement come from the same geographic area as his predecessor). So, casting around, President Madison decided on Alexander Wolcott of Connecticut.

Wolcott came from one of Connecticut's most distinguished families, and he was a Republican. There were factors against him as well, however. During the Jefferson administration, Wolcott had been the chief enforcer—in Connecticut—of the hated embargo of 1807 (which had been intended to hurt the British but failed in that regard). Adding to his unpopularity was the fact that Wolcott also had little legal experience. He was nominated, and his name went to the U.S. Senate, where it was rejected by the crushing number of 24 to 9. This was the single most lopsided rejection ever handed by Congress to a nominee to the Supreme Court.

Exasperated, President Madison tried yet again. He submitted the name of John Quincy Adams (son of President John Adams) to the Senate. John Quincy Adams came from a Federalist family, but he was at that moment a moderate Republican. He was well regarded by men of both parties, and his nomination was quickly passed by a unanimous vote in the Senate. There was only one problem—Adams declined to serve.

John Quincy Adams was in Russia, serving as America's ambassador to Czar Alexander I, when he received the news of his nomination. He promptly declined, sending a letter saying he did not wish to leave the political field for the judicial one. This was one of the more honest replies ever to come from a person who declined a Supreme Court appointment. As things turned out, John Quincy Adams did go on in politics, and in 1824 he was elected the sixth president of the nation. He never became a justice of the Supreme Court, however.

President Madison waited a few months before he tried again. By then, Judge Samuel Chase had died, and there were *two* vacancies on the high Court. In November 1811, President Madison submitted the names of Joseph Story of Massachusetts and Gabriel Duvall of Maryland to the Senate. Both men were confirmed within three days.

At 32, Joseph Story was the youngest man ever to be nominated and confirmed to the high Court. He was delighted, as he indicated in a letter to a friend:

> My Dear Friend,
>
> So far as my judicial duties go, I find myself considerably more at ease than I expected. My brethren are very interesting men, with whom I live in the most frank and unaffected intimacy. Indeed, we are all united as one, with a mutual esteem which makes even the labors of jurisprudence light.[22]

Story and the other six justices lived together in a boardinghouse in Washington, D.C. Since the Supreme Court met only from the first of February until the middle of March, it would have been a great burden for each of the justices to maintain his own residence. Instead, they lived rather like college students, except that they were older men and wiser ones. Story had this to say about sitting on the Supreme Court bench:

> The mode of arguing cases in the Supreme Court is excessively prolix and tedious; but generally the subject is exhausted, and it is not very difficult to perceive at the close of the cause, in many cases, where the press of the argument and of the law lies. We moot every question as we proceed, and my familiar conferences at our lodgings often come to a very quick, and I trust, a very accurate opinion in a few hours.[23]

Very likely it was John Marshall who first shepherded the justices into living together in one boardinghouse. This proximity allowed him to exert his great charm and persuasion on his fellow judges.

Appointed by James Madison, Joseph Story was the youngest associate justice of the Supreme Court. Story was an important member of John Marshall's court and was involved in many of the decisions that bolstered a strong federal government.

A few weeks later Story wrote to his wife:

My Dearest Wife:

It will probably take me twelve days to reach home after I set out on the journey. I fear the roads in New England are now very bad, and I shall rest a little on the road if it is practicable.

Two of the Judges are widowers, and of course objects of considerable attraction among the ladies of the city. We have fine sport at their expense, and amuse our leisure with some touches at match-making. We have already ensnared one of the Judges, and he is now (at the age of forty-seven) violently afflicted with the tender passion. Being myself a veteran in the service, I take great pleasure in administering to his relief, and I feel no small pride in remarking that the wisdom of years does not add anything of discretion to the impatience, jealousies, or doubts of a lover.

The breakfast bell has just rung; it was quite musical to my ears this morning, although on other occasions its loud tones are harsh and ungenial.

Your affectionate husband, Joseph Story.[24]

Joseph Story would come, over time, to know those New England roads very well. He was assigned the first—or New England—judicial circuit riding district, and there would be many years during which he would travel about 1,500 miles (2,414 km) on horseback or in a carriage.

WAR BEGINS

The War of 1812 began the same year that Story took his place on the high Court. The two stories are not connected in any major way, but we continue to use his writing, and wit, to illuminate the United States in this time of war.

President Madison was far from being a warmonger, but by June 1812 he had had enough. The British had been impressing U.S. sailors for roughly a decade, with no end in sight. Madison was also pressured by the youthful "War Hawks" in Congress; they wanted to start a war in order to have a reason to capture and hold British Canada. Even Thomas Jefferson, in retirement at Monticello, wrote that Canada seemed to be theirs for the marching.

Madison made his official request on June 1, and Congress approved the declaration of war on June 18. By a most remarkable twist of irony and fate, however, the British Parliament decided to abandon the policy of impressments six weeks earlier. This move did neither side any good, though, for it took six weeks for a ship to reach the United States with the news, and by then the war had begun in earnest.

IMPRESSMENT

After 200 years, we are still astonished by the nerve of the British Royal Navy. How did the British dare to steal American sailors off their merchant vessels?

The answer lies in the power of the British navy. In the first and second decades of the nineteenth century, His Majesty's Navy was just about as powerful as the United States Air Force is today. No other nation had a navy even remotely as powerful as did King George III.

Beginning around 1803, British naval ships routinely stopped American merchant vessels on the high seas. A British officer would come aboard the American ship and demand to speak to each member of the crew. Often, the British officer would say that two or three of the men he had examined turned out to have English accents, and to seem as if they were British by birth. The British had a long-standing policy "once an Englishmen always an Englishman," and they therefore *pressed* these men into service in the British Royal Navy. The United States protested but could do nothing about it.

In 1807, President Jefferson announced an economic embargo against Great Britain, but it harmed American merchants more than the British. By the time James Madison came into office as the fourth president, nearly 5,000 Americans had been stolen from their ships and were now serving in the British navy. The great question was: Would America go to war with England over this matter?

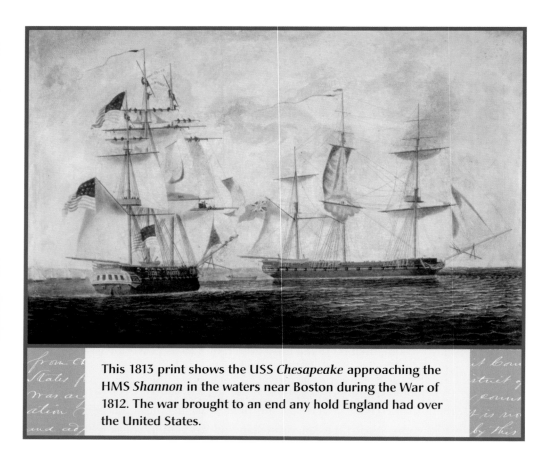

This 1813 print shows the USS *Chesapeake* approaching the HMS *Shannon* in the waters near Boston during the War of 1812. The war brought to an end any hold England had over the United States.

Americans began the war flush with enthusiasm. Like the Sage of Monticello, as Jefferson was now called, they believed that 7½ Americans could defeat and conquer a mere 500,000 British Canadians. The British began, not with enthusiasm, but with confidence. They felt sure the great Royal Navy would control America's coast and keep "Brother Jonathan" (as they called Americans) at bay. Both sides were wrong.

Not only was the British-Canadian resistance stronger than expected, but also the British and their Indian allies won a major victory, capturing Fort Detroit. The timid old commander of Detroit, General William Hull, was a Revolutionary War veteran; he was intimidated by the way the British and Indians marched and countermarched around his position. General

Hull did not know that the British and Indians were using a local woods to recirculate their men, making it seem they had more than was the case. General Hull and 2,000 Americans surrendered without a fight. This was the most disgraceful loss of American troops of the nineteenth century.

Just days later, however, the Americans won a stunning victory at sea. USS *Constitution* met and crushed HMS *Guerriere* off the Nova Scotia coast; the American ship won its nickname, "Old Ironsides," from its performance in this battle. The British were winning on land and the Americans were winning at sea, but things were about to change.

THE DARKEST TIME

America and Britain were fairly evenly matched in 1813. Generally, the British did better at sea, though the Americans continued to win many ship-to-ship contests, and the Americans did better on land. They recaptured Fort Detroit and defeated the British and their Indian allies at the Battle of the Thames River in Ontario. The great Indian leader Tecumseh was killed in the battle.

The darkest time for America came in the summer of 1814, however. Finally, the British were able to use all their resources in the struggle. Until the spring of 1814, they were fighting the Americans on one side of the ocean and Napoleon Bonaparte on the other. The French emperor abdicated his throne in April 1814, though, and went off into retirement and exile on the Mediterranean isle of Elba. Now Great Britain was able to use everything it had against the United States.

The British public was alarmed over the American ship-to-ship victories and wanted to see the United States given a good thrashing. About 30,000 first-line British troops crossed the ocean to chastise the Americans. In August 1814, the British landed 3,000 of their best troops in Maryland. These men, led by General Robert Ross, moved rapidly toward the U.S. capital, which was less defended in summer than at other times. Many congressmen chose to leave the city during the sweltering summer months.

President James Madison and First Lady Dolley Madison were in Washington, but they were unable to affect the

WASHINGTON'S PORTRAIT

The story has been told many times, but it loses nothing in the telling. First Lady Dolley Madison is credited with saving the now-famous life-sized portrait of George Washington executed by Gilbert Stuart.

President James Madison had left the capital to observe the Battle of Bladensburg. After the American defeat, his advisors would not let him return to Washington and risk capture. He sent word to his wife to leave swiftly and join him in the countryside. Dolley Madison wanted to go quickly; she did not wish to be captured. At the last minute, however, she took another look at the magnificent full-length painting of George Washington and decided it must not fall into the enemy's hands.

The painting was too large and heavy to be packed, so an axe was brought forth and the gold frame broken. The painting was rolled up like a scroll. Then, and only then, would the First Lady allow herself to be taken from the President's House (they did not call it the White House yet).

Dolley and James Madison both evaded capture. They spent several days in the countryside, then returned to Washington, D.C. Her heroism in saving the portrait made the couple much more popular to average Americans. They could not occupy the President's House, though, because it had been badly damaged by fire. It was rebuilt over the next three years, and, because of its fresh shiny paint, it became known as the White House.

outcome. The American militia force was routed by the British at the Battle of Bladensburg, and the British reached Washington late on the afternoon of August 24. The British stayed in Washington less than 24 hours, but they burned as many buildings as they could. American pride was injured, but its banks and financial system were hurt even worse.

All through the summer of 1814, banks had increasingly paid out less in gold, silver, and copper coin (better known as specie). As soon they learned Washington, D.C., had been taken, all the banks south and west of New England suspended specie payments entirely. Americans had their paper notes, but they could not get the precious metals upon which those notes were based. A run on the banks had been preempted.

America was in very bad financial straits in the second half of 1814. Many congressmen may have regretted having "killed" the BUS back in 1811, for it was the only institution that could have helped the country through this financial crisis. The national debt soared to about $124 million; this at a time when the annual national budget was about $18 million. Indeed, if it were not for the much-maligned foreigners, the United States might not have weathered the storm.

Earlier, we saw that suspicion of foreigners and foreign influence played a major role in bringing down the Bank of the United States. But in 1814, the actions of a handful of foreign-born Americans were all that stood between the nation and financial breakdown. Stephen Girard of Philadelphia (a Frenchman by birth) lent millions to the U.S. government. Secretary of the Treasury Alexander Dallas (born in Jamaica and educated in England) was a powerful force for good in the national affairs. A man of great energy and talent, he drew up plans for what might become a second Bank of the United States. John Jacob Astor (born in Germany but now a New Yorker) was a major investor in U.S. securities. He also believed a new BUS was necessary. The "foreigners" helped keep the nation going in 1814.

PEACE AND VICTORY

Just when it seemed that things couldn't get worse, things began to get better. In the autumn of 1814, Congress considered
a national draft for the first time in American history. As things
turned out, such a draft became unnecessary. Just six months
after the burning of Washington, D.C., Justice Joseph Story
wrote an uplifting and optimistic letter to a friend in Baltimore:
"Peace has come in a most welcome way to delight and aston-
ish us. Never did a country occupy more lofty ground; we have
stood the contest, single-handed, against the conqueror of Eu-
rope; and we are at peace, with all our blushing victories thick
crowding on us."[25]

Victories? In September 1814, just a month after the burning of Washington, the people of Baltimore successfully re-
pulsed a British attack. In that same month, a British fleet and
army on Lake Champlain were turned back by American forces.
In addition, most remarkably of all, shortly afterward, in early
1815, General Andrew Jackson and his coalition of Southern
frontiersmen, New Orleans merchants, and Barataria Bay pi-
rates thrashed the British at the Battle of New Orleans. Story
continued, "Never was there a more glorious opportunity for
the Republican party to place themselves permanently in power. They have now a golden opportunity; I pray God that it may
not be thrown away."[26]

Joseph Story was a Republican, but he was a New England
Republican, as the words he wrote to his friend attest:

> Let us extend the national authority over the whole ex-
> tent of power given by the Constitution. Let us have great
> military and naval schools; an adequate regular army; the
> broad foundations laid of a permanent navy; a national
> bank; a national system of bankruptcy; a great navigation
> act; a general survey of our ports, and appointments of port
> wardens and pilots; judicial courts which shall embrace the
> whole constitutional powers; national notaries; public and

national justices of the peace, for the commercial and national concerns of the United States.[27]

Joseph Story was very clearly a loose constructionist when it came to the Constitution, meaning that, like Alexander Hamilton, he believed the Constitution was "elastic" enough to allow for things not specifically written by the Founding Fathers. He continued:

> By such enlarged and liberal institutions, the Government of the United States will be endeared to the people, and the factions of the great States will be rendered harmless. Let us prevent the possibility of a division, by creating great national interests, which shall bind us in an indissoluble chain.
>
> Believe me as ever, Your affectionate friend, Joseph Story.[28]

Seldom has anyone ever laid out such a broad and sweeping view of what the United States could and should do. Remarkably, much of what he called for would eventually come to pass.

7

The Problems
of Peace

The results of the U.S. Victory in the War of 1812 were mixed. There is no doubt that Americans were pleased to have the war over. Though they did not know it, this was the last time they would fight the British; the next time the two countries fought, it would be as allies in World War I. Certain concerns, especially financial ones, worsened, though, even as the war ended. One of the major issues was the "dumping" of cheap British goods.

The British had the largest economy in the transatlantic region. Their merchants eagerly cut prices to entice American consumers, and British goods soon undercut American ones.

The competitive situation was described by Hezekiah Niles, editor of *Niles' Weekly Register*, published in Baltimore:

> There are very few "thinking people" in the United States
> of forty years old and upwards that have not remarked the
> wonderful change which has taken place in manners and
> habits amongst us, within the last thirty years. The progress
> of luxury and extravagance has been unparalleled—and in-
> deed, the present generation regards the last as having had a
> sort of antediluvian [before the flood] character.[29]

Niles said he could remember when a dish of souchong tea
would have been an incredible luxury. He pointed out, however:
"Reformation and retrenchment are much easier preached than
practiced. There is something extremely unpleasant and severe
in the idea of denying ourselves the luxuries we have enjoyed."[30]
Everyone knows this truth. It is hard to back away from the
things to which one has become accustomed, and Americans
found it difficult to turn away from the low-priced luxuries the
British offered, even if they were British.

As he so often did, Niles took a broad sweep at banks in
general: "The evils to be apprehended from the profuse habits
of the people will be powerfully assisted in their ulterior effects
by the monied aristocracy which the same artificial state gave
rise to—I mean our BANKING INSTITUTIONS."[31]

Niles was on the right track, but he missed some of the
point. New banks were springing up because there was a sense
of prosperity in the land. Niles was right in saying that this prosperity would have to be reined in eventually; he was three years
ahead of the Panic of 1819. He was mistaken in thinking that
the banks were the cause of American problems, though; the
trouble was simply that the British turned out cheaper goods,
and American consumers wanted to buy them.

In the last paragraph of his essay on "Reform and Retrenchment," Niles turned his attention to the British: "Let us

banish from our houses all useless articles of foreign man-
ufacture, and substitute the buck-skin like cloths and stout
cottons of our own country for the flimsey goods sent from
England, particularly made for the American market."[32] Even
if Niles succeeded in convincing Americans to cease buying
foreign goods, it was too late to stop the thing he considered
the greatest evil. The Bank of the United States was about to
have a second incarnation.

THE SECOND BUS

As soon as the War of 1812 ended, energy in Congress began to
develop for a new Bank of the United States. In financial terms,
the country had limped, badly, through the war. The national
debt was at an all-time high, banks were in disfavor (until about
1815), and the persistent distrust of foreigners such as Stephen
Girard and Alexander Dallas helped poison economic matters.
Toward the end of 1815 and in the spring of 1816, however,
Congress made some dramatic moves, and President Madison
signed the bill creating the second BUS.

Like the first BUS, the new Bank was given a 20-year charter, to run from 1817 to 1837. Like its predecessor, the second
BUS would have its headquarters in Philadelphia, and there
would be a number of branch banks. Like the first BUS, the
second would have a great deal of federal money in its coffers,
but it would be a private institution, operating apart from the
U.S. government.

President Madison signed the bill that created the kind of
institution his mentor Thomas Jefferson had so much feared
and disliked. Jefferson still lived in retirement at Monticello.
Americans listened with reverence to many of his opinions, especially those on agriculture and architecture, but in matters of
finance he seemed like a man who had lived beyond his times.
The peaceful, agrarian republic for which he had argued in 1791
seemed far away indeed.

YEAR WITHOUT A SUMMER

The year the Bank came back to life, 1816 is best known to Americans as the year without a summer. Actually, it is known to Europeans for the same ghastly weather. The year began normally enough, but early in June there was a strong snowfall that blanketed New England. Spring crops were ruined, and people scrambled to adjust.

The Fourth of July was celebrated with gusto, but just three days later came another major snowfall: This one was mixed with ice. The second plantings were ruined, and many New Englanders contemplated moving westward. (It was around this time that a major westward emigration to Ohio and Indiana began.)

At about the same time, the southern and western states endured a period of dryness and drought. Crops were spoiled, and fewer American goods made it to market that year. Few Americans actually went hungry; the young nation was a veritable bread basket, even in hard times. Many Americans, however, did fear that the weather had taken an unprecedented turn for the worse.

Luckily, the weather improved in 1817. Memories of the "Year Without a Summer" began to fade, and it was not until modern times that the reason was discovered. The immense Tambora Volcano in Indonesia erupted in 1815, sending dust particles around the world, blocking sunlight, and causing cooler conditions in many areas, including the United States.

INFLATION AND PAPER MONEY

The U.S. economy seemed to boom in 1817 and 1818. "Seemed" is the right word, for much of the growth was based on an inflationary spurt, created by the enthusiasm following the end of the War of 1812. Americans bought more and bought faster than ever before.

The opening of western lands was one reason for the inflation. As soon as the war was over, Americans resumed their

GROWTH OF BANKS AND BANKING

The following chart shows a remarkably fast growth of banks in the two decades that followed the "death" of the first Bank of the United States.[*]

State	1811	1815	1820	1830	Broken Banks
MA	15	21	28	66	6
ME	6	8	15	18	2
NH	8	10	10	18	2
RI	13	4	30	47	1
VT			1	10	
NY	8	26	33	37	10
NJ	3	11	14	18	7
PA	4	42	36	33	16
DE		5	6	6	1
MD	6	17	14	13	9
DC	4	10	13	9	4
VA	1	4	4	4	0
NC	3	3	3	3	2
SC	4	5	5	5	2
GA	1	2	4	9	1
LA	1	3	4	4	2
AL			3	2	3
MS		1	1	1	
TN	1	2	8	1	9
KY	1	2	42	--	43
OH	4	12	20	11	20
IN			2		2
IL			2		2
MO			1		2
MI				1	1
FL				1	
	83	188	299	317	147

[*] Gouge, William M. *A Short History of Paper Money and Banking in the United States*. Philadelphia: T.W. Ustick, 1833, p. 61.

westward migrations, which now reached well into the Ohio and Mississippi river valleys. Hundreds of thousands of Americans poured into the western states, buying up public (federal) land at the remarkably cheap price of $1.60 per acre.

This growth was made possible by paper currency. In 1817 and 1818, American banks printed an excess of paper notes, and many Americans wondered if the days of specie (or hard

Southern politician John C. Calhoun began his career as a nationalist and eventually changed course to become a proponent of states' rights. Along with Henry Clay, he favored war with Britain and then worked to build a national bank and other centralized federal institutions.

money) would ever return. Many did not mind the shift to paper (which Hezekiah Niles called "rag"), but that was because they had not felt the crunch.

NEW CONGRESSIONAL LEADERS

By 1816, the year the second Bank of the United States (BUS) was created, the old revolutionary leaders were almost entirely gone. Men who had been in their twenties during the Revolution were now in their sixties, and many of them had been through physical hardships in the war that had shortened their lives. Henry Clay, John C. Calhoun, and Daniel Webster were the outstanding leaders of the new, young generation.

Born in Virginia, Henry Clay moved to Kentucky in his youth. He became Speaker of the U.S. House of Representatives in 1810 and was a major "War Hawk," helping to bring on the War of 1812. When the war was over, Clay became a key spokesman for the American System—a connected system of roads, canals, and markets to bring the products of the western states to the eastern ones.

Born in South Carolina, John C. Calhoun was a nationalist in his youth and an extreme states' rights defender in his old age. Calhoun favored creating the new BUS in 1816; indeed, he was a primary force in the congressional debates that led to it.

Born in New Hampshire, Daniel Webster had already come to be identified with the interests of New England as a whole. A staunch Federalist, he might have been expected to welcome the creation of a second BUS, but the party lines had blurred by 1816 to the point that some Republicans were for it and many Federalists, like Webster, were against it.

President James Madison might have been expected to oppose bringing the Bank back to life. The events of the War of 1812, however, had persuaded him of the necessity of the institution.

Once the United States had moved to using paper bills, the variety was seemingly endless. The above image illustrates the denominations used in the late eighteenth century.

It began in the summer of 1818. The Bank of the United States had a president and 20 members of the board of directors. Many of them became concerned in the spring and summer of 1818. They noted the vast outpouring of paper money around the nation, and the relative scarcity of specie, meaning silver, gold, or copper coins.

William Jones, president of the BUS, had been a good politician during the War of 1812, but he was miscast as the nation's financial regulator. Jones did not see the trend until it was too late. In the summer of 1818, the BUS's central branch at Philadelphia began to restrict credit and to hoard specie in its vaults. The Panic of 1819 was about to begin. Before it commenced, however, the BUS suffered another shock. The state of Maryland had the audacity to tax it.

MCCULLOCH AND MARYLAND

James W. McCulloch is a rather mysterious figure. He appears in the public record as the collector for the port of Baltimore around 1812, then as the cashier for the Baltimore branch of the Bank of the United States. By 1817, McCulloch was cashier for the Baltimore branch. Sometime that year he entered into cahoots with James Buchanan and William Smith, two of the most respected merchants of Baltimore and Philadelphia, respectively. The three men decided to rob the BUS blind.

At first it was easy. As cashier, McCulloch could make loans to himself and his partners. Individually, each of the three men then purchased more BUS stock, seeking to drive it artificially higher. When the right moment came, they could sell all their shares at a tremendous profit. That moment never came.

In February 1818, the Maryland legislature decided to tax the BUS. Maryland began to print a set of paper sheets on which the Baltimore branch would have to make out its paper money. The use of the special paper was a tax in and of itself; if the BUS wanted to avoid the nuisance of dealing with the paper, it could pay a flat tax of $15,000 per year. James McCulloch and the Baltimore branch would not pay. This brought on the great Supreme Court case. It was not the only great and important case argued that year, however.

8

Lawyers and Arguments

Everyone in Washington, D.C., expected that the Supreme Court session of 1819 would be especially important. Not only would the *Dartmouth v. Woodward* case be decided, but the *McCulloch v. Maryland* case would be argued, and there was yet another important case in *Sturges v. Crowninshield*.

The cases were all quite different on an individual level, but collectively they added up to a discussion and debate on American nationalism itself. What power did the federal government have relative to that of the states? Could the states employ whatever powers had not been granted to the federal government in the Constitution? Did individuals have the right to seek economic redress from the states, or could they only petition the federal government? All these issues had to be argued and decided.

As usual, Hezekiah Niles weighed in on the major questions: "Neither time nor room is allowed to us this week to express our views of the course that is warranted, or the State of the case requires us to pursue, and in respect to the bank of the United States, further than to say that we are for the *middle ground*—to restrain the power, but not to destroy the institution. Feb. 6, 1819."[33] Just one week later, Hezekiah Niles spoke again:

> We think that the bank ought to be preserved—but that, as the opportunity is fitting, its immense power to do mischief should be restrained. He must be a dolt, indeed, who does not see that it may become a political machine, to make all officers—from the president of the United States down to the very scavengers of an incorporated town: and that, if it cannot attain such power, it will exercise it, he is undeniable—unless its directors be "angels in the form of men"—and seek truth rather than speculation. February 13, 1819.[34]

Niles was clearly in favor of Maryland's right to tax the bank:

> The best restraining power that we can discover is—in an acknowledged right in the states to tax it. THE PEOPLE ARE THE ONLY SAFE DEPOSITORY OF THEIR OWN INTERESTS. If it does well, it will be permitted to exist, with its branches; if it does ill, it may, after a reasonable time allowed to wind up its affairs, be driven from any of the states. That the states have a right to tax it, I cannot hesitate to believe—or, their sovereignty is as nothing.[35]

Niles had spoken. Now it was up to the Court to listen.

Founding Father Luther Martin *(above)* refused to sign the Constitution because he felt it was a dangerous step away from states' rights. Martin served as the defense attorney in two important U.S. legal cases, Aaron Burr's treason trial and Samuel Chase's impeachment trial, before arguing on behalf of the state of Maryland in the Supreme Court case *McCulloch v. Maryland*.

John Marshall knew that *McCulloch v. Maryland* might be the single most important case of his long judicial career. To prevent any sense of impropriety, Marshall sold his 100-plus shares of the Bank of the United States weeks before the case began.

Given the importance of the case, Marshall also declared that the Court would suspend some of its usual rules. Most plaintiffs and defendants were limited to two lawyers and a short argument period for each, but Marshall allowed both sides to have as many lawyers as they wished.

Daniel Webster came forward as an attorney for the BUS. As a congressman, in 1816, he had voted against the creation of the BUS. Now he saw the importance and value of the Bank. William Pinckney also argued for the Bank. Pinckney was considered the greatest lawyer of his time. Had he not died when he was in his forties, his reputation might have been as great as that of Daniel Webster. William Wirt, a former solicitor general for the United States, also argued for the BUS. Wirt did not have the oratorical flourishes of either Webster or Pinckney, but he was a solid lawyer.

Maryland also sought the best and brightest. First it turned to Luther Martin. Born in 1745, Martin was a decade older than John Marshall, and about 30 years older than some of his opposing attorneys. He had practiced law longer than some of them had lived. Martin had an interesting, and complex, reputation. Many who heard him considered him a lawyer with the greatest mind of the past 30 years. Without referring to notes, he could cite precedent upon precedent from memory. He had his critics, too, however. A decade earlier, the young congressman Joseph Story had heard Luther Martin argue in front of the Supreme Court and told a friend: "His dress is slovenly. You cannot believe him a great man. Nothing in his voice, his action, his language impresses. Of all men he is the most desultory, wandering, and inaccurate."[36] It was well known that Martin had a drinking problem. One reason he was still arguing cases at such an advanced age was that although he had earned plenty of money in his long life, he had spent most of it, too.

DARTMOUTH V. WOODWARD

No more arguments had been made in this case. Everything had been said in March 1818. On February 4, the day the Court opened for session, John Marshall pulled a 17-page-long handwritten opinion from the sleeves of his black robe. He began to read. The Court's opinion was long, but its essence can be ascertained rather quickly. Marshall and the Court found that: (1) Dartmouth was a private, charitable, and benevolent institution. (2) The state of New Hampshire had tried to take Dartmouth over. (3) The effort was in error because of the charter of 1769. Marshall and the Court ruled that the charter of 1769 was a contract in the proper sense of the word.

Those in favor of the *Dartmouth* case have pointed to it, ever since, as a great moment in the defense of private institutions. This is certainly true, but it was also a stretch on the part of Marshall and the Court. Almost certainly, the Court gave a unanimous opinion because of its bias in favor of unrestrained rights of property.

STURGES V. CROWNINSHIELD

This case seemed, and still seems today, like a very small matter, and not a case for the Supreme Court. In 1811, Richard Crowninshield of Massachusetts, then living in New York, borrowed money from William Sturges. Within months of signing the IOU, Cronwinshield was off the hook because of a New York state law that prevented the collection of debts.

Making the case truly interesting, and of significant moment for the Court, was the fact that Crowninshield was from the Crowninshields of Salem, Massachusetts, one of America's richest families. One of their members had been secretary of the

U.S. Navy, and the family had been instrumental in launching Joseph Story's career. Story should have recused himself from the case, but he did not.

Marshall spoke, again for a unanimous Court: Article 1 of the Constitution specifically gave Congress the power to handle matters of bankruptcy, even when there were different states involved. Therefore, Crowninshield could not escape his debt, which had to be paid to Sturges. This seems like such a small matter, but it emphasized, once more, the adherence of the Marshall Court to nationalism. There are those who say that John Marshall's entire career was devoted to American nationalism and the economic strength of the federal government, but perhaps more specifically:

> His great nationalist opinions, in McCulloch, Gibbons, and Dartmouth College aimed to create not a *nation-state* but a national market, an arena in which goods and credit moved without hindrance across state lines. Such a market, if the Court could fashion one from the raw material of the Constitution and the pressing needs of a new class of entrepreneurs, would provide an arena where enterprising individuals operating according to common-law principles of contract could put their creative energies to work for themselves and for their country. Contractual freedom and contractual responsibility, guaranteed by the rule of law was the thread that united Marshall's multifaceted jurisprudence.[37]

How, then, would he rule in *McCulloch v. Maryland*?

THE GREAT CASE

The case began in February 1819. With *Dartmouth v. Woodward* and *Sturges v. Crowninshield* behind him, John Marshall went to work on the biggest case he had seen since *Marbury v. Madison*, in 1803.

First, the Court had the Maryland law read. In 1818, the state of Maryland announced that every bank must purchase its special stamps for its paper bills or pay a general fine. Opponents of

 NECESSARY AND PROPER CLAUSE

The U.S. Constitution grants many powers to its bicameral (two-chamber) legislature. Congress has the power to tax, although all bills involving taxes must originate in the House of Representatives (this was taken from the British system in which only the House of Commons can initiate tax legislation). Congress can also create militias, raise armies and navies, and do all sorts of things such as create a post office, a system of bankruptcy, and so forth. Nowhere in the Constitution, however, does it mention that Congress has the power to create a bank of any type.

Thomas Jefferson had pointed this out in 1791. His memoranda to President George Washington on the subject became the basis for the arguments of many states' rights supporters throughout the country. Washington had found in favor of Alexander Hamilton, though, who was the first to use the necessary and proper clause to win an argument: "The Congress shall have power to . . . make all laws which shall be necessary and proper for carrying into execution the foregoing powers, and all other powers vested by this Constitution in the government of the United States, or in any department or officer thereof."*

Alexander Hamilton was the first to give this argument in a state paper. John Marshall and his Court were the first to use it to decide a number of law cases. The necessary and proper clause has become a hallowed part of U.S. legal philosophy.

---

*That is article 1, section 8 of the U.S. Constitution.

Maryland had already protested that this amounted to a second Stamp Act upon the United States. Everyone knew what happened when Great Britain had tried to put a stamp act on the colonies in 1765.

Once the Maryland law was on the table, arguments began. Daniel Webster led off for the Bank of the United States. Webster had already made his reputation the previous year, with his arguments in the *Dartmouth* case. He may have felt even stronger about this case, given his strong support for nationalistic causes, but he did not employ as many oratorical flourishes as before:

> Steam frigates, for example were not in the minds of those who framed the Constitution, as among the means of naval warfare; but no one doubts the power of Congress to use them, as means to an authorized end. It is not enough to say that it does not appear that the bank was in the contemplation of the framers of the Constitution. It was not their intention in these cases to enumerate particulars.[38]

Webster was arguing in favor of the necessary and proper clause. He went on:

> *Necessary* powers must here intend such powers as are *suitable* and *fitted* to the object; such as our *best* and *most useful* in relation to the end proposed. If this be not so, and if Congress could use no means much such as were *absolutely indispensable* to the existence of a granted power, the government would hardly exist; at least it would be wholly inadequate to the purposes of its formation. A bank is a proper and suitable instrument to assist the operations of the government.[39]

Webster argued that corporations were always means, and not ends in themselves. Since the Bank of the United States was simply a means to an end, Congress had the proper authority to create it. Webster probably knew that he was preaching to the converted. At least three members of the high Court (Marshall, Washington, and Story) were firm and committed nationalists. But Webster also knew that he had to win over some of the other judges.

The second question was, if the bank was constitutionally created, did the state governments have power to tax it? Webster clearly believed that they did not:

> If the states may tax the bank, to what extent shall they tax it, and where shall they stop? *An unlimited power to tax involves, necessarily, a power to destroy;* because there is a limit beyond which no institution and no property can bear taxation. Our question of constitutional power can hardly be made to depend on a question of more or less. If the states may tax, they have no limit but their discretion; and the bank therefore must depend on the discretion of the state governments for its existence [italics added].[40]

Webster was using a well-known legal trick. Maryland had not attempted to tax the BUS out of existence; it simply tried to obtain some revenue from the existence of the Baltimore branch. Webster was arguing that a worst-case scenario would necessarily mean the bank would be driven out of every state in the nation.

He was not entirely wrong. Ohio and Kentucky were at that moment contemplating legislation to bring about taxes against the BUS. Webster concluded by pointing out that the BUS held its charter from the federal government. If the states could drive the BUS out, they would be depriving the federal government of one of its major powers. Webster was impressive that day, but his speech did not "make" his reputation in the same way that his arguments had in the Dartmouth case a year before.

A REBUTTAL

Joseph Hopkinson spoke for the State of Maryland:

> The argument might have been perfectly good, to show
> the necessity of a bank for the operations of the revenue
> in 1791, and entirely fail now, when so many facilities for
> money transactions abound, which were wanting then. . . .
> [N]ecessity was the plea and justification of the First Bank
> of the United States. If the same necessity existed when the
> second was established, it will afford the same justification;
> otherwise it will stand without justification, as no other
> is pretended.[41]

He made a good point. There were about *three* banks in the
entire United States when the first BUS was created in 1791. No
one had an exact count of how many banks existed in 1819, but
it was suggested there were well over 300.

Hopkinson argued against the BUS on the grounds that it
was a monopoly:

> In truth, the directors have exercised the power, and they
> hold it without any control from the government of the
> United States; and as is now contended, without any con-
> trol of the state governments. A most extravagant power to
> be vested in a body of men, chosen annually by a very small
> portion of our citizens, for the purpose of loaning and trad-
> ing with their money to the best advantage![42]

Hopkinson also attacked the idea that banks should be free
from taxes: "There is nothing in the nature of the property of
bank stock to exonerate it from taxation. It has been taxed, in
some form, by every state in which a bank has been incorpo-
rated; either annually and directly, or by a gross sum paid for
the charter."[43]

He concluded with a flourish: "It might as well be said
that a tax on real estate, imposed after a sale of it, and not
then perhaps contemplated, or new duties imposed on

Federalist congressman Joseph Hopkinson argued against the BUS on the grounds that it was a monopoly, calling it "a most extravagant power to be vested in a body of men . . . for the purpose of loaning and trading with their money to the best advantage!"

merchandise after it is ordered, violates the contract between the vendor in the purchaser, and diminishes the value of the property."[44]

AN ATTACK

Luther Martin then argued for Maryland. He was the oldest man in the courtroom, a full decade older than John Marshall. Despite the deprecating remarks made about him by Joseph Story, Luther Martin was indeed the most venerable member of the American bar. He had been the attorney general of Maryland for 35 years and had now come out of semiretirement to argue the *McCulloch* case.

Martin had gone through many twists and turns in life. In 1788, he had been opposed to the new Constitution, because it did not do enough to protect the rights of states. Then, in the 1790s, he changed completely and became so Federalist in his opinions that Thomas Jefferson once referred to him as the bull dog of the Federalist Party. Martin knew his chances of success were slim—he knew John Marshall and the spirit of the Marshall Court—but, he would do his best.

Martin began by reading several tracts from the *Federalist* and from the debates of the Virginia and New York conventions. These documents had been written roughly 30 years before, at a time when Americans were deciding whether to accept or reject the work of the Founding Fathers. John Marshall showed some apprehension as Luther Martin began to read, for Martin used some of Marshall's own words from the Virginia convention of 1788.

Responding to Patrick Henry, Marshall had posed several rhetorical questions: "Does the government of the United States have the power to make laws on every subject?" Marshall denied that the Constitution gave Congress such powers. "Can they go beyond the delegated powers?" He again answered no. If they were to make a law not warranted by any of the powers enumerated, Marshall concluded, it would be considered by the judges as an infringement of the Constitution, which they are to guard.[45] Luther Martin went on for some many hours, but he had already delivered his best argument.

PINCKNEY TO THE RESCUE

William Pinckney was the most distinguished leader of the American bar in 1819. Born in Pennsylvania, he had worked his way up through life the hard way (as John Marshall had), and he had little patience for those without his internal fortitude. Everyone admitted Pinckney was one of the greatest speakers of the day and that his arguments were usually lucid, but he had earned the enmity of many of his colleagues. Playing to the judge, and sometimes to the female observers in the audience, Pinckney often slighted his fellow attorneys. This was not one of those days, however.

The clerk's recording of Pinckney's argument makes it seem as though he followed in the path of Daniel Webster and laid out a strictly rational argument. One can use Justice Joseph Story as a secondary source, though. He was amazed by Pinckney's eloquence that day:

> My dear brother
>
> Mr. Pin[c]kney arose on Monday to conclude the argument; he spoke all that day and yesterday, and will probably conclude today. I never, in my whole life, heard a greater speech; it was worth the journey from Salem to hear it; his elocution was excessively vehement, but his eloquence was overwhelming. . . . All the cobwebs of sophistry in metaphysics about states rights and state sovereignty he brushed away with a mighty [broom]. We have had a crowded audience of ladies and gentlemen; the hall was full almost a suffocation and many went away for want of room. I fear that the speech will never be before the public, but if it should be, it will attract universal admiration. Mr. Pinckney possesses, beyond any man I ever saw, the power of elegant and illustrative amplification.[46]

All arguments had been given. The decision was now in the hands of seven men in black robes.

9

Opinion and Justification

S adly, almost nothing is known about how the Marshall Court reached its decision. There are no handwritten notes, no tell-tale descriptions of how Marshall and his colleagues decided on their opinion. There is no way to know what Bushrod Washington, Gabriel Duval, and the other members of the high Court thought on the matter.

What *is* quite clear is that the wording, language, and tone of that decision came straight from John Marshall. Some scholars have questioned his ability to write such a long opinion in just three days; they suggest he may have written it much earlier. Later efforts in writing for the newspapers, however, show that Marshall was a prodigious worker, who could turn out a great deal of copy when he wanted to. John Marshall read the Court's opinion on March 6, 1819. He read to his fellow judges, the court reporters, and the fairly large crowd that had gathered to hear this important decision.

Noting that this was an occasion of great importance, Marshall said, "No tribunal can approach such a question without a deep sense of its importance, and of the awful responsibility involved in its decision."[47] The first crucial question he addressed was: Did Congress have the power to create a bank?

To many in the audience, the answer was simple. There was no mention of the word "bank" in Article I, which delineated the powers of Congress. Marshall noted, however, that there had been extensive arguments at the time of the bank's creation (in 1791) and that none of the objections had been strong enough to prevent its coming into form at that time. He had to grant that the original BUS of 1791 had been allowed to expire, in 1811, but he pointed out that "a short experience of the embarrassments to which the refusal to revive it exposed the government, convinced those who were most prejudiced against the measure of its necessity."[48]

Without fully answering the question he had posed, Marshall looked back to 1787, the year 55 men had come to Philadelphia to write a new constitution. He rebuffed the idea that it was the 55 men or even the constitutional conventions of each state that had truly ratified the document. Marshall put forth the idea that it was, quite simply, the people of the 13 states who had done the deed: "The government proceeds directly from the people; is ordained and established in the name of the people; and is declared to be ordained in order to form a more perfect union, establish justice, ensure domestic tranquility, and secure the blessings of liberty."[49] What mattered, Marshall said, was that the people had made the final decision; the Constitution was not forced upon them by the states (indeed, nothing could be forced upon the people, as they were the sovereign power in the land).

Marshall poked fun at those who tried to make him repent his words from 1788: "The counsel for the state of Maryland have deemed it of some importance, in the construction of the constitution, to consider that instrument, not as emanating from the people, but as the act of sovereign and independent states."[50] He did not have to remind anyone that he had been one of those chosen to debate the virtues and defects of the Constitution back in 1788. In other words, the states were intermediaries at best. The PEOPLE had accepted the CONSTITUTION, and it was now the law of the land.

Having made some strong statements, Marshall now took a step back: "Among the enumerated powers [of Congress] we do not find that of establishing a bank or creating a corporation."[51] In these 17 words, Marshall seemed to admit that the lawyers for the State of Maryland were correct. He went on, however: "A constitution, to contain an accurate detail of all the subdivisions of which its great powers will admit, and all the means by which they may be carried into execution, would partake of the prolixity of a legal code, and could scarcely be embraced by the human mind. It would, probably, never be understood by the public."[52] Marshall did not give ordinary Americans much credit!

Marshall went on, "In considering this question, then, we must never forget that it is a *constitution* we are expounding.[53] These 17 words are the ones most often quoted when legal scholars discuss the *McCulloch v. Maryland* decision. Marshall put his finger right on the crux of the issue, saying that a constitution could not spell out each and every fact and detail: that something had to be left to the people—like himself—who had the power to interpret or expound the document.

Marshall then used one of the ideas of Daniel Webster (who had spoken of steam frigates) and referred to the post office. Article I of the Constitution gave Congress the power to create a post office and post roads. Nothing was said, however, of postal employees or of methods for guarding and carrying the mail. Did this mean Congress could not take such actions? Of course not. Perhaps Marshall had this in mind because there indeed had been several recent major thefts of the mail, especially that between New York and Philadelphia.

Finally, Marshall gave his explicit view, and that of the Court: Congress had the authority to create a bank. Alexander Hamilton would have been happy. It had taken a full 30 years for the Supreme Court to test his brainchild, the Bank of the United States, and it had been found constitutional.

THE POWER TO TAX; THE POWER TO DESTROY

Marshall proceeded to the second great question: Could Maryland tax the BUS?

This required some looking back into the constitutional growth of the nation. Everywhere he looked, Marshall saw precedents for the power of federal taxation. At no point or place did he see precedent for state taxation of federal institutions. Everything Marshall had said so far now built to his grand conclusion:

> The result is a conviction that the states have no power, by taxation or otherwise, to retard, impede, burden, or in any manner control the operations of the constitutional laws enacted by congress to carry into execution the powers vested in the general government. We are unanimously of opinion, that the law passed by the legislature of Maryland, imposing a tax on the Bank of the United States, is unconstitutional and void.[54]

PUBLIC RESPONSE

The response to the decision was strong and sometimes furious. Hezekiah Niles was one of the first to weigh in. Agreeing

The decision in the *McCulloch v. Maryland* case (*above*) was delivered on March 6, 1819. John Marshall ruled in favor of the constitutionality of the federal government to create a national bank and denied states the right to tax the federal government.

that the *McCulloch* decision was one of the most important of recent times, he lamented that the Supreme Court acted like "a tribunal so far removed from the people that some seem to regard it with a species of that awful reverence in which the inhabitants of Asia look up to their princes."[55] Niles announced his intention to print a series of editorials titled "Sovereignty of the States" (as usual, he was as good as his word). Yet Niles's response was kind compared to some responses. Southern newspapers, especially, were appalled by the decision.

It was Marshall himself who decided to carry out a preemptive strike. He wrote to Joseph Story, saying that the two of them, and the rest of the Supreme Court, would be damned by the whole country if they did not speak up for themselves. Marshall did not indicate what he would do, but, given his skill with the pen and the written word, it is likely he had already decided to answer back in print.

NEWSPAPER BATTLES

Marshall was right. Just days after he wrote to Joseph Story, the first major article came out in the *Richmond* [Virginia] *Enquirer.*

Richmond was Marshall's hometown, but his was a classic case of the Biblical axiom that prophets are not honored in their home areas. For nearly three decades, Marshall had been an outspoken Federalist in a town and state that revered its states' rights heritage. His beliefs had not precluded him from being elected a congressman, back in the 1790s, but one sincerely doubts he could have won a hometown election for anything at the time of the *McCulloch* decision. The *Richmond Enquirer* ran the following opinion written by "*Amphictyon*":

> I confess, that as a citizen, I should have been better pleased to have seen the separate opinions of the judges. The occasion called for *seriatim* [separate written] opinions. On this great constitutional question, affecting very much the

rights of the several states composing our confederacy, the decision of which abrogated the law of one state, and is supposed to have formed a rule for the future conduct of other states, the people had surely a right to expect that each judge should assign his own reasons for the vote which he gave.[56]

It is difficult to argue with this assertion. In its first decade, the Supreme Court made a point of issuing seriatim opinions. The public had been able to see, in *Chisholm v. Georgia*, exactly how each justice had arrived at his decision. Not so with *McCulloch*.

Once again we can thank (or curse) John Marshall for an important change. The practice of issuing seriatim opinions had been on the decline before he took over as chief justice in 1801, but once he arrived it virtually disappeared. Marshall wanted the Court to speak with a unified voice. *Amphictyon* then took aim at Marshall: "That his opinion is very able, every one must admit. This was to have been expected, proceeding as it does from a man of the *most profound legal attainments*, and upon a subject which has employed his thoughts, his tongue, and his pen, as a politician, and an historian, for more than thirty years [italics added]."[57]

These were broad swipes at the chief justice. Not everyone knew, perhaps, that Marshall's entire legal education consisted of a summer of classes at the College of William and Mary. The use of the word *politician* was surely pejorative, for Supreme Court judges were not supposed to have political opinions. Most important of all, however, was the way Marshall had trampled on the rights of the states. *Amphictyon* built his argument around the manner in which the U.S. Constitution had been approved, back in 1788: "Who gave birth to the constitution? . . . the states themselves in their highest political, and sovereign authority; by whose separate conventions, representing, not the whole mass of the

After *McCulloch*, John Marshall continued to lead important decisions on the Supreme Court. In addition, he remained active in state and federal politics and worked to resettle freed slaves in Africa. As chief justice for six presidential terms, Marshall participated in more than 1,000 Supreme Court decisions.

population of the United States, but the people only within the limits of the respective sovereign states, the constitution was adopted and brought into existence."[58]

Again, it is difficult to argue with the proposition. *Amphictyon*, however, suffered from the same handicap endured by nearly all those who argue in favor of states' rights. Language works better for those who argue for nationalism: "The United States *are*" used to be the common expression. After the Civil War, the expression changed to "the United States *is*." Even before the guns of the Union army had won their point, though, Americans tended to favor the simple, direct language of nationalism over the difficult and sometimes tortured language of states' rights. It is simply much easier to say "one nation, indivisible" than it is to say "50 states, linked by a common bond."

Amphictyon went on to decry the bold assertion of powers that Marshall had made in favor of the federal government. The author of *Amphictyon* clearly saw that the *McCulloch* case had ramifications far beyond those contained within the Bank of the United States or even the currency as a whole. At a time when the legislatures of states such as New York and Indiana were pushing for canals, roads, and eventually railroads, which would transform transportation and commerce, Marshall had struck a mighty blow in favor of the federal government having the ultimate say in the matter.

Marshall felt compelled to respond. As mentioned earlier, Marshall and Bushrod Washington were so close that people often considered them "one judge" in two bodies. Washington was on circuit duty in Pennsylvania when Marshall sent him a swift answer to *Amphictyon*. Titled *A Friend to the Union*, Marshall's response ran first in the Philadelphia newspapers and then spread to other parts of the country. Unfortunately, the Philadelphia editor took it on himself to rearrange the wording and sequence of *A Friend to the Union*, so the words never took on their characteristic Marshall-like strength. Thanks to the efforts of legal historian Gerald Gunther, however, we have the words today in their proper sequence.

Marshall began by decrying the necessity to argue such a point in the newspapers. The business of the Court, he said, was to make legal decisions, not to have to explain them in the media. Marshall then took on the question of seriatim opinions. This had been a point of controversy for many years. During the tenure of John Jay and Oliver Ellsworth (who had been chief justices from 1790 to 1800), all members of the Supreme Court had written their own, individual, decisions on each major case. This practice had stopped during Marshall's tenure, and he now found it necessary to defend his practice. Marshall pointed out that the unified decision presented in the *McCulloch* case was the work of the entire Court, not just the chief justice. Never before had Marshall felt it necessary to defend his work in this manner. He then took on the major points *Amphictyon* had raised:

> I will proceed to consider the first objection made to the opinion of the Supreme Court. It is stated to be "the denial that the powers of the federal government were delegated by the states."
>
> This assertion is literally not true. The court has not, in terms, denied "that the powers of the federal government were delegated by the states," but has asserted affirmatively that it "is emphatically and truly a government of the people," that it "in form and in substance emanates from them."[59]

Marshall and *Amphictyon* were never going to agree on this crucial point. Marshall and those who believed in federalism thought that the people of the original 13 states had collectively created and approved the Constitution. Amphictyon and those who believed in states' rights, or confederation, believed it was the people of the 13 states, *in their individual states*, who had created the Constitution, and therefore the nation. Marshall concluded:

I have now reviewed the first number of *Amphictyon*, and will only add my regrets that a gentleman whose claims to our respect appear to be by no means inconsiderable should manifest such excessive hostility to the powers necessary for the preservation of the Union, as to arraign with such bitterness the opinion of the supreme court on an interesting, constitutional question.[60]

There were more newspaper battles to come, but *Amphictyon* and *A Friend to the Union* had drawn the lines. Americans could choose for themselves.

Short-term 10 and Long-term Effects

When evaluating the results of the *McCulloch* decision, it is useful to consider the most quoted words of John Marshall from that decision: "We must never forget that it is a *constitution* we are expounding." In other words, a constitution is not like a menu or a list of goods. It is created by its founders for very specific reasons, but those reasons may become out of date. A constitution must evolve organically in order to endure.

Marshall may not have used those words precisely, because he knew the deep attachment most Americans had to the "founding moment" of 1787. Marshall, however, gifted lawyer though he was, was never a slave to that founding moment.

Born in 1755, he was only 32 when the Constitution was written. Thanks to good health, he lived to the age of 79, and in that time he witnessed great changes in American society and economics. More than most people realized, John Marshall was a thoroughgoing pragmatist. He would change with the times, when necessary.

It was precisely this ability to change with the times that made Marshall, generally speaking, superior to many of those around him. Thomas Jefferson had a deeper mind, with more varied interests, and Alexander Hamilton had been unsurpassed in his ability with facts and figures. These men, however, great as they were, lacked Marshall's ability to hold to a specific concept—that of a strong federal government—and to apply all sorts of different reasons for doing so. To say he infuriated his foes is an understatement. From his retirement at Monticello, Thomas Jefferson lamented the way the federal government had fallen under the spell of this "crafty chief judge," who did what he wanted when he wanted.

At the time it was issued, *McCulloch* was considered one of the most important decisions the Supreme Court had rendered. Over the course of time, though, it would come to be seen as more than important. *McCulloch* is still seen today as a defining moment in the long battle between federal and state governments over the issue of sovereignty.

THE PANIC OF 1819

Today we call them recessions or depressions, but in the nineteenth century, they were called "Panics." There was the Panic of 1819, the Panic of 1837, and the Panic of 1857. Each time, there was a run on the banks because people lost confidence in the currency, or in the banks' ability to secure their deposits.

Shares of BUS stock sagged to as low as $95 a share. They had been as high as $150 a year earlier. That was only the beginning, however. Many small state and local banks closed their doors. By law, they were required to send a large amount of their specie (silver, gold, and copper) east to the main branch of the BUS. This crippled many of them, forcing them to go into receivership. Americans living in the western states discovered

JOHN MARSHALL'S AUTOBIOGRAPHY

In 1827, at the age of 62, John Marshall sat down to write a short autobiographical sketch. All evidence suggests he would not have done so if he was not prompted, and prompted severely, by his friend Joseph Story.

Throughout a long life, Joseph Story remained a keen, even a fervent, admirer of John Marshall. Story first met Marshall in 1808. The two men served together on the Court from 1811 to Marshall's death in 1835. Late in their friendship, Joseph Story urged Marshall to write something about his early life. Marshall answered:

> The events of my life are too unimportant, and have too little interest for any person not of my immediate family, to render them worth communicating or preserving. I felt therefore some difficulty in commencing their detail, since the mere act of detailing, exhibits the appearance of attaching consequence to them—a difficulty which was not overcome till the receipt of your favor of the 14th instant. If I conquer it now, it is because the request is made by a partial and highly valued friend.*

Readers can be glad that Joseph Story wore John Marshall down and persuaded him to write down some basic facts and thoughts. Even so, they rusted away in a private collection for a century and were only made available to the public in 1937.

*John Stokes Adams, ed. *Autobiographical Sketch by John Marshall.* Ann Arbor: University of Michigan Press, 1937, p. 3.

In an attempt to bring the opposing parties closer after the War of 1812, James Monroe ushered in the so-called Era of Good Feelings. Monroe did not place much emphasis on the national economy, instead focusing on foreign policy.

how dependent they had become on the loose and easy credit offered from 1816 to 1818. As credit contracted, Americans stopped buying the public lands in Indiana and Illinois, leading to a decrease in the revenues of the federal government. Many

Americans, especially those in southern and western states, were furious. They believed they had been duped by John Marshall and the Supreme Court. If only the Court had allowed Maryland to tax the BUS! In the short term, *McCulloch* was important, even provocative. In the long run, it was decisive.

PRESIDENT MONROE

James Monroe was the last of the "Virginia Dynasty" of presidents that commenced with Thomas Jefferson. Monroe was a conscientious public servant, but, like many leading politicians of the time, he thought the economy was not the responsibility of the president or the executive branch. When he gave his annual address to the American people (the "State of the Union" was given in December in those days), President Monroe spoke at great length about American relations with Spain and the recent purchase of Florida, but he had only this to say about the Panic of 1819, which had crippled the finances of hundreds of thousands of people:

> The causes which have tended to diminish the public receipts, could not fail to have a corresponding effect upon the [federal] revenue which has accrued upon imposts and tonnage during the first three quarters of the present year. It is, however, ascertained that the duties which have been secured during that period, will exceed $18,000,000 and those of the whole year will probably amount to $23,000,000.[61]

The federal government had enough money to keep going, but did the people?

AFTER THE PANIC OF 1819

It has long been difficult to determine how many people were affected by the Panic of 1819 and to what extent. Recent research suggests, however, that Americans were affected to the core, because the Panic of 1819 was a great dividing point between their agrarian past and their fiscal and industrial future.

As for the players in the period leading up to the Panic, John Marshall died peacefully in 1835, just a bit shy of his eightieth birthday. The Liberty Bell in Philadelphia cracked while tolling for his passing.

Joseph Story lived on until 1845. He was heartbroken that President Andrew Jackson did not choose him as the new chief justice after Marshall's death: That post went to Roger Taney of Maryland.

Hezekiah Niles was thrown from a horse in 1835. Injured and later paralyzed by a stroke, he turned over leadership of the *Weekly Register* to his son, who sold the newspaper six months after his father's death in 1839.

James McCulloch, James Buchanan, and William Smith were indicted for larceny, but they never served jail time. The laws of the United States had not yet been designed to handle matters of embezzlement, and the three men escaped on technicalities.

What about the Bank of the United States?

DEATH OF THE BANK

Andrew Jackson won the presidential election of 1828. Not coincidentally, this was only the second time that Americans came out to choose their electors; before this, there had been very few popular votes. Born in South Carolina, Jackson had moved to Tennessee as a young man. Long before he became President, Jackson was identified with the interests and beliefs of *western* Americans, those on the other side of the Appalachian Mountains. When he came to Washington, D.C., for his inauguration, Jackson brought with him a large crowd of western supporters.

John Marshall was still alive in 1829. He administered the oath of office to Andrew Jackson, just as he had done for every incoming president since 1801. Marshall must have known that Andrew Jackson was different, though—that his presidency would bring about great changes.

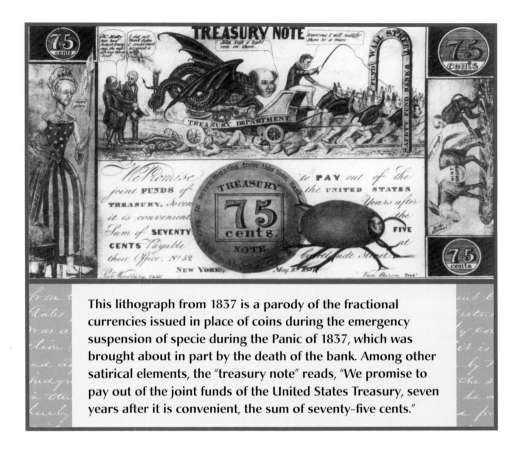

This lithograph from 1837 is a parody of the fractional currencies issued in place of coins during the emergency suspension of specie during the Panic of 1837, which was brought about in part by the death of the bank. Among other satirical elements, the "treasury note" reads, "We promise to pay out of the joint funds of the United States Treasury, seven years after it is convenient, the sum of seventy-five cents."

Jackson started fast; that was his style. By 1830, he had pushed through a bill to move all Indians to the west of the Mississippi River. By 1832, he was running for reelection and he was fighting John C. Calhoun over matters of states' rights versus federal sovereignty (as usual, Jackson prevailed). In that same year, he cast a veto that "killed" the Bank of the United States. Just as in 1811, when the BUS sought a second charter, Jackson struck it down, claiming that the Bank was the refuge of monied scoundrels.

Jackson had firm support among a cadre of western congressmen, men who remembered the Panic of 1819. Foremost among them was Thomas Hart Benton. The Missouri senator was called "Old Bullion" for his belief in specie and dislike for paper currency. On several occasions, Benton gave a speech for which he became famous. Describing the BUS and the economic horrors it had created, he called the Bank a devouring beast and said, "All the flourishing cities of the West are mortgaged to the moneyed power. They may be devoured by it at any moment. They are in the jaws of the monster! A lump of butter in the mouth of a dog! one gulp, one swallow, and all is gone!"[62]

Jackson enjoyed great public support. One of the most popular books of the day described the Panic of 1819 and the extraordinary measures taken to keep the BUS afloat: "The Bank was saved and the people were ruined. For a time, the question in Market Street, Philadelphia, was, every morning, not who had broken the previous day, but who yet stood. In many parts of the country, the distress was as great as it was in Philadelphia, and in others it was still more deplorable."[63]

The veto had major consequences. Congress was unable to muster the two-thirds vote needed to override, and the BUS went out of existence in 1836. Jackson had done this in the name of the people, but the people then suffered during the Panic of 1837, which was partly brought about by the death of the Bank of the United States.

Americans as individuals tended to do just fine without a national bank, but the economy and fiscal system suffered until 1862, when the greenback was made the official currency of the United States. One can say that the issue of having a national bank or not was not fully settled until 1913, the year the Federal Reserve Board was created. (Every dollar issued today has the words "Federal Reserve Note" engraved on the top.)

CONSTITUTIONAL ISSUES AND LEGAL IMPLICATIONS

As important as the financial considerations were, the constitutional and legal ones were even greater. *McCulloch* was

The Federal Reserve was created in response to three major economic panics during times when there was no centralized banking system. Its main responsibilities are to regulate the nation's banks, maintain the stability of the economy, and moderate interest rates. Even today, the system has its critics.

issued in 1819, a time when the United States was at a crossroads. Would the nation remain a loosely affiliated set of states, spread over the eastern seaboard? Or would the country become a mighty federal republic, which stretched to the Mississippi and beyond? There is no doubt where John Marshall stood on the issue. In *McCulloch* he said:

> Throughout this vast republic, from the St. Croix [in Maine] to the Gulf of Mexico, from the Atlantic to the Pacific, revenue is to be collected and expended, armies are to be marched and supported. The exigencies of the

nation may require that the treasure raised in the north should be transported to the south, that in the east, conveyed to the west, or that this order should be reversed. Is that construction of the constitution to be preferred which would render these operations difficult, hazardous and expensive?[64]

For better or worse, John Marshall and the Supreme Court ruled in favor of American nationalism and against the idea of states' rights. We have lived with the consequences ever since.

Chronology

1755   John Marshall is born in Virginia.

1775   The Revolutionary War begins; John Marshall enlists.

1777   Hezekiah Niles is born in Pennsylvania.

1779   Joseph Story is born in Massachusetts.

1780   Marshall has a short legal education at the College of William & Mary.

1781   The war ends with an American victory at Yorktown.

1782   Daniel Webster is born in New Hampshire.

1787   Constitutional Convention attendees write the new U.S. Constitution.

1788   Marshall argues in favor of adopting the new Constitution. The Constitution becomes the law of the land.

1789   George Washington becomes the first president. The first Congress meets.

1790   The first Supreme Court meets in New York.

1791   Congress charters the Bank of the United States (BUS).

1792   The federal government moves to Philadelphia.

1793   The Court rules in *Chisholm v. Georgia*.

1795   The states push through the Eleventh Amendment in response to *Chisholm*.

1797   George Washington leaves public life. John Adams becomes the second president.

1798   John Marshall is involved in the XYZ Affair with France.

1800   Marshall becomes the secretary of state. John Adams fails to win reelection.

1801   Marshall is nominated and confirmed as chief justice. Thomas Jefferson wins the presidential election with a runoff in U.S. House of Representatives. Marshall administers the oath of office to his distant cousin.

1803 Marshall hands down the opinion in *Marbury v. Madison*.

1805 The impeachment trial of Justice Samuel Chase takes place.

1808 Congressman Joseph Story visits the Marshall Court.

1809 James Madison becomes the fourth president of the United States.

1811 Congress decides not to recharter the BUS. Bank of Stephen Girard takes its place. A new group of young congressmen take over. Two vacancies on the high Court are filled by Joseph Story and Gabriel Duvall.

Timeline

1755
John Marshall is born in Virginia.

1791
The Bank of the United States (BUS) is chartered by Congress.

1755

1803

1790
The first Supreme Court meets in New York.

1803
Marshall hands down the opinion in *Marbury v. Madison*.

1812   The War of 1812 begins. Story and Duvall take their places on the Court.

1813   The war brings both victory and defeat.

1814   Washington, D.C., burns. Most American banks suspend redemption of paper money by specie. Congress contemplates a national draft.

1815   Battle of New Orleans. America is euphoric. British merchants begin to dump cheap goods on American consumers.

1816   Americans feel the climatic effects of a volcanic eruption in Indonesia, experiencing a cold summer and the disruption of crops. The second BUS is established by Congress.

1814
Washington, D.C., burns. Most American banks suspend redemption of paper money by specie. Congress contemplates a national draft.

1819
Congress debates the value of the BUS. Arguments are heard in *Sturges v. Crowninshield* and *McCulloch v. Maryland*. McCulloch and others are indicted in Maryland. The Panic of 1819 sets upon the people and the economy.

1814   **1837**

1816
The second BUS is established by Congress.

1837
The United States suffers its second major financial panic.

1817   Westward migration picks up pace. The BUS extends credit on an easy basis.

1818   Arguments are heard in *Dartmouth v. Woodward*. The BUS begins to tighten credit and call in loans.

1819   The president of BUS resigns. Suspicion of the BUS Baltimore branch develops. John Marshall sells his BUS stock. Congress debates the value of the BUS. John Marshall delivers the Court opinion in *Dartmouth v. Woodward*. Arguments are heard in *Sturges v. Crowninshield* and *McCulloch v. Maryland*. Marshall gives the Court opinion in both cases. Marshall defends his opinion in anonymous newspaper articles. McCulloch and others are indicted in Maryland. The Panic of 1819 sets upon the people and the economy.

1821   The United States begins to recover from the Panic of 1819.

1827   Joseph Story persuades Marshall to write his autobiographical sketch.

1828   Andrew Jackson becomes the seventh president of the United States.

1832   Jackson vetoes the new charter for the BUS.

1833   William Gouge's essay against the banks is published.

1835   John Marshall dies. Roger Taney becomes the new chief justice.

1837   The United States suffers its second major financial panic.

1839   Hezekiah Niles dies.

1845   Joseph Story dies.

Notes

Chapter 1

1. Irons, Peter. *A People's History of the Supreme Court.* New York: Penguin Books, 1999, p. 127.
2. Baxter, Maurice G. *Daniel Webster & The Supreme Court.* Amherst, Mass.: University of Massachusetts Press, 1966, p. 84.

Chapter 2

3. Merriam-Webster. *Webster's Ninth New Collegiate Dictionary.* Springfield, Mass. 1989.
4. Herbert A. Johnson, ed. *The Papers of John Marshall* (vol. 1). Chapel Hill, N.C.: University of North Carolina Press, 1974, p. 256.
5. Ibid., p. 259.

Chapter 3

6. U.S. Constitution, reproduced in Peter Irons, *A People's History of the Supreme Court.* New York: Penguin Books, 1999, p. 491.
7. Ibid.
8. *The Supreme Court of the United States: Its Beginnings & Its Justices 1790–1991.* Commission on the Bicentennial of the United States Constitution, 1992, p. 15.
9. Ibid., p. 16.

Chapter 4

10. Bowman, John S., ed. *Facts About the American Wars.* New York: H.W. Wilson, 1998, p. 126.
11. John Stokes Adams, ed. *Autobiographical Sketch by John Marshall.* Ann Arbor, Mich.: University of Michigan Press, 1937, p. 29.
12. Ibid., p. 30.

Chapter 5

13. William W. Story, ed., *Life and Letters of Joseph Story: Associate Justice of the Supreme Court of the United States, and Dane Professor of Law at Harvard University* (2 vols). Boston: Little, Brown, 1851, p. 166.
14. Ibid., pp. 166–167.
15. Ibid., p. 167.
16. Ibid.
17. Ibid., pp. 167–168.
18. Ibid., p. 168.

19. Ibid.
20. Ibid.

Chapter 6

21. Adams, Henry. *History of the United States of America during the Administrations of James Madison*, p. 229.
22. Story, *Life and Letters of Joseph Story*, p. 215.
23. Ibid., pp. 215–216.
24. Ibid., p. 219.
25. Ibid., p. 254.
26. Ibid.
27. Ibid.
28. Ibid.

Chapter 7

29. *Niles Weekly Register*, October 16, 1816.
30. Ibid.
31. Ibid.
32. Ibid.

Chapter 8

33. *Niles Weekly Register*, February 6, 1819.
34. Ibid., February 13, 1819.
35. Ibid.
36. Story, *Life and Letters of Joseph Story*, p. 164.
37. Newmyer, R. Kent. *John Marshall and the Heroic Age of the Supreme Court*. Baton Rouge, La.: Louisiana State University Press, 2001, p. 271.
38. Wheaton, Henry. *Reports of Cases Argued and Adjudged in the Supreme Court of the United States* (6 vols). Philadelphia: J. Grigg, 1830–1834, pp. 320–321.
39. Ibid., p. 324.
40. Ibid., pp. 324–325.
41. Ibid., pp. 331–332.
42. Ibid., p. 335.
43. Ibid., p. 339.
44. Ibid., p. 352.
45. Irons, Peter. *A People's History of the Supreme Court*. New York: Penguin Books, 1999. pp. 123–124.
46. Story, *Life and Letters of Joseph Story*, p. 325.

Chapter 9

47. Savage, David G. *Guide to the U.S. Supreme Court*. Washington, D.C.: CQ Press, 2004, p. 1071.
48. Ibid.
49. Ibid.
50. Ibid.
51. Ibid., p. 1072.
52. Ibid.
53. Ibid.
54. Ibid, p. 1078
55. Ibid, p. 1075.
56. Gunther, Gerald, ed. *John Marshall's Defense of McCulloch v. Maryland*. Palo Alto, Calif., Stanford University Press, 1969, p. 53.
57. Ibid., p. 54.
58. Ibid., pp. 55–56.
59. Ibid., p. 78.
60. Ibid., p. 80.

Chapter 10

61. *Niles Weekly Register,* December 11, 1819.
62. Smith, Elbert B. *Magnificent Missourian: The Life of Thomas Hart Benton.* Philadelphia: J.B. Lippincott, 1958, p. 127.
63. Gouge, *A Short History of Paper Money and Banking in the United States,* p. 32.
64. Savage, *Guide to the U.S. Supreme Court,* p. 1072.

Glossary

despotism A government by a singular, absolute authority.

dissenting opinion A written opinion by a judge or judges who disagree with the minority opinion.

Federalist A member of the early U.S. political party that favored a strong centralized federal government.

impressment The policy of forced recruitment by the British Royal Navy in the eighteenth and nineteenth centuries.

mercantilism An economic and political philosophy that stresses the development and control of tradable goods (or commodities) as a means to foster the general good or wealth of a society or country.

partisan Supporting a cause or party.

recuse To disqualify oneself from a legal case.

seriatim In a series, one after another.

souchong A fine quality of tea.

sovereignty The right to exercise supreme control over something.

states' rights As outlined by the Constitution, the rights of individual states—rather than the federal government—to have power over certain matters.

Bibliography

Adams, Henry. *History of the United States of America During the Administrations of James Madison.* New York: Library of America, 1986.

Adams, John Stokes, ed. *Autobiographical Sketch by John Marshall.* Ann Arbor, Mich.: University of Michigan Press, 1927.

Anthony, David. "Gone Distracted: Sleepy Hollow, Gothic Masculinity, and the Panic of 1819." *Early American Literature* 40:1 (2005): 111–144.

Catterall, Ralph C.H. *The Second Bank of the United States.* Chicago: University of Chicago Press, 1903.

Gouge, William M. *A Short History of Paper Money and Banking in the United States.* Philadelphia: T.W. Ustick, 1833.

Gunther, Gerald, ed. *John Marshall's Defense of* McCulloch v. Maryland. Palo Alto, Calif.: Stanford University Press, 1969.

Hobson, Charles F., ed. *The Papers of John Marshall.* Chapel Hill, N.C.: University of North Carolina Press, 1995.

Irons, Peter. *A People's History of the Supreme Court.* New York: Penguin Books, 1999.

Luxon, Norval Neil. Niles' Weekly Register: *News Magazine of the Nineteenth Century.* Baton Rouge, La.: Louisiana State University Press, 1947.

Newmyer, R. Kent. *John Marshall and the Heroic Age of the Supreme Court.* Baton Rouge, La.: Louisiana State University Press, 2001.

Newmyer, R. Kent. *Supreme Court Justice Joseph Story: Statesman of the Old Republic.* Chapel Hill, N.C.: University of North Carolina Press, 1985.

Olson, Sherry H. *Baltimore: The Building of an American City.* Baltimore, Md.: The John Hopkins University Press, 1980.

Rodell, Fred. *Nine Men: A Political History of the Supreme Court from 1790 to 1955.* New York: Random House, 1955.

Rothbard, Murray N. *The Panic of 1819: Reactions and Policies.* New York: Columbia University Press, 1962.

Savage, David G. *Guide to the U.S. Supreme Court*. Washington, D.C.: CQ Press, 2004.

Smith, Elbert B. *Magnificent Missourian: The Life of Thomas Hart Benton*. Philadelphia: J.B. Lippincott, 1958.

Story, William W., ed. *Life and Letters of Joseph Story: Associate Justice of the Supreme Court of the United States, and Dane Professor of Law at Harvard University* (2 vols). Boston: Little, Brown, 1851.

Webster, Fletcher, ed. *The Private Correspondence of Daniel Webster*. Boston: Little, Brown, 1857.

Wheaton, Henry. *Reports of Cases Argued and Adjudged in the Supreme Court of the United States* (6 vols). Philadelphia: J. Grigg, 1830–1834.

Further Reading

Hubbard-Brown, Janet. *How the Constitution Was Created*. New York: Chelsea House, 2007.

Irons, Peter. *A People's History of the Supreme Court*. New York: Penguin Books, 1999.

Niles' Weekly Register (1811–1845). Found in bound volumes in specialized libraries.

Rodell, Fred. *Nine Men: A Political History of the Supreme Court From 1790 to 1955*. New York: Random House, 1955.

Shnayerson, Robert. *The Illustrated History of the Supreme Court of the United States*. New York: Abrams, 1986.

Wagner, Heather Lehr. *The Supreme Court*. New York: Chelsea House, 2007.

Picture Credits

8: Library of Congress Prints and Photographs Division

12: Library of Congress Prints and Photographs Division

14: Michael Sheldon/Art Resource, NY

17: National Archive and Records Administration

21: Getty Images

26: National Archive and Records Administration

28: Réunion des Musées Nationaux/ Art Resource, NY

31: National Archive and Records Administration

33: Library of Congress Prints and Photographs Division

36: Library of Congress Prints and Photographs Division

38: National Archive and Records Administration

42: National Archive and Records Administration

44: Getty Images

49: National Archive and Records Administration

53: Library of Congress Prints and Photographs Division

54: The Granger Collection, New York

56: The Granger Collection, New York

59: Réunion des Musées Nationaux/ Art Resource, NY

61: The Granger Collection, New York

63: National Portrait Gallery, Smithsonian Institution/Art Resource, NY

67: Library of Congress Prints and Photographs Division

70: Library of Congress Prints and Photographs Division

80: National Portrait Gallery, Smithsonian Institution/Art Resource, NY

81: Library of Congress Prints and Photographs Division

83: HIP/Art Resource, NY

87: The New York Public Library for the Performing Arts/Music Division/Artres

95: The New York Public Library for the Performing Arts/Music Division/Artres

102: National Archive and Records Administration

105: National Portrait Gallery, Smithsonian Institution/Art Resource, NY

112: Library of Congress Prints and Photographs Division

115: Library of Congress Prints and Photographs Division

117: © Lance Nelson/CORBIS

Cover: The Granger Collection, New York

Index

About the Author

Samuel Willard Crompton lives and works in the Berkshire Hills of western Massachusetts. A prolific historian and biographer, he has written about 40 books on topics as diverse as lighthouses, spiritual leaders, and decisive battles. He is a major contributor to the *American National Biography*. Work on this 24-volume compendium has provided the inspiration for many of his ventures into new areas and topics.

About the Editor

Tim McNeese is an associate professor of history at York College in York, Nebraska. A prolific author of books for elementary, middle school, high school, and college readers, McNeese has published more than 80 books and educational materials over the past 20 years on subjects such as Alexander Hamilton to the siege of Masada. His writing has earned him a citation in the library reference work, *Something about the Author*. In 2005, his textbook *Political Revolutions of the 18th, 19th, and 20th Centuries* was published. Professor McNeese served as a consulting historian for the History Channel program *Risk Takers, History Makers.*